Teddy Bears,
Toys & Tales

Teddy Bears, Toys & Tales

Jean Greenhowe

A DAVID & CHARLES CRAFT BOOK

ACKNOWLEDGEMENTS

The designs in this book were originally featured in *Woman's Weekly* magazine and the author would like to express her thanks to the editor and home department staff for their assistance and co-operation.
The author and publishers also wish to thank IPC Magazines, publishers of *Woman's Weekly,* for their kind permission to reproduce their photographs.

British Library Cataloguing in Publication Data

Greenhowe, Jean
  Teddy bears, toys & tales.
  1. Soft toys. Making
  I. Title
  745.592'4

  ISBN 0-7153-9367-7

Photographs on pages 69, 103 © Jean Greenhowe
All other photographs © IPC Magazines

Toys, text and patterns © Jean Greenhowe 1990

Typeset by Typesetters (Birmingham) Ltd
Smethwick, West Midlands
and printed in Portugal
by Resopal
for David & Charles Publishers plc
Brunel House Newton Abbot Devon

Distributed in the United States by
Sterling Publishing Co Inc
387 Park Avenue South, New York, NY 10016-8810

Contents

INTRODUCTION 7

GENERAL TECHNIQUES 8

TWO TUBBY TEDDIES 14

THE CAMELS 20

NURSERY-TALE TEDDIES 25
  Wee Teddy Winkie
  Little Bear Riding Hood
  Cinderbearella
  Robear-in-Hood

ISABELLA 33

SANTA AND MRS CLAUS 45

BEST-DRESSED BEAR 50

OCEANS OF TOYS 56

HUMPTY DUMPTY 62

SOFT TOPS 68

SLEEPING BEAUTY AND THE PRINCE 75

ZOO RUG 83

LITTLE BOY BLUE AND LITTLE BO-PEEP 92

SIMPLE CHIMPS 96

FOUR BEARS 101

FOUR FURRY TOYS 107

WILD WEST SHOW 115

CLOWN 122

STOCKISTS 127

ENGLISH-AMERICAN GLOSSARY 127

INDEX 128

Introduction

If you enjoy making toys, then this collection is guaranteed to bring hours of pleasurable sewing. There are designs for a wide variety of toys, ranging from a large sit-upon camel to activity toys such as a zoo playrug complete with tiny animals and children. And of course there are the ever-popular teddy bears, large and small, and some with surprising personalities!

Each character is brought to life with an original story or rhyme and I hope that adults as well as children will find them entertaining. So start sewing now, and great fun will be had by one and all!

General Techniques

It is worth taking time to read through the following notes and the instructions for each toy before making a start on any design, so that you are familiar with what is involved. If the instructions are then followed carefully, your toy should turn out just like the one shown in the illustration.

MATERIALS AND EQUIPMENT

Safety first
With regard to safety, common sense is needed when using any materials to make toys for children. It is obvious that very young children and babies should not be given toys which contain potentially dangerous items such as buttons, beads, wire or any other parts which could cause injury or become detached and swallowed.

Adhesive
When adhesive is called for in the instructions, use an all-purpose type such as UHU, unless another kind of glue is mentioned. To remove the odd unwanted smear of UHU on fabric, felt or trimmings, use a small piece of cloth dipped in acetone and dab until the acetone dissolves and removes the glue. Take care when using acetone as it is highly inflammable. It can be obtained from any pharmacist's.

Dressmaking equipment
You will need all the ordinary items as used for dressmaking – sewing machine, sewing threads, sharp scissors (both large and small pairs), sewing needles, tape measure, thimble and so on.

Ruler
Use a ruler marked with metric and imperial measurements.

Pins
Large glass or plastic-headed pins are the best kind to use when making soft toys, as they are much easier to see and handle than ordinary pins. To avoid the danger of any pins being left in the toy accidentally, use a limited number and count them at each stage of making.

Tweezers
These can be very useful when handling small pieces of fabric or felt – for example, when glueing facial features in place. Tweezers can also be used to turn very small pieces right side out after stitching, and for stuffing.

Compasses
A pair of inexpensive school compasses are invaluable for drawing out small circular patterns. Very large circles outside the span of your compasses can easily be drawn as described in the section headed Copying the Patterns (page 9).

Old Scissors
It is a good idea to keep an old pair of scissors just for cutting card and paper because these will blunt your good scissors.

Strong thread
This is occasionally required for gathering, when the gathers in thick fabrics or stuffed shapes have to be pulled up very tightly. Buttonhole thread is the type to use. Although this is available in various colours, it is not always necessary to have thread which matches the fabric if it will be covered eventually by other materials or trimmings. White is best for general purposes.

Stuffing
There are many types of man-made fibre filling available for toy-making which are suitable for the designs in this book, and all of them are washable. To give some idea of the variety, here is a list from a current catalogue (see list of stockists). All these fillings con-

form to British standards for health and safety.

Polydown For use where an up-market luxurious soft touch is required. Fully carded to produce bulk without weight.

Super A top grade white polyester fibre, fully carded to give enormous bulk. Soft and springy, use to give your toys that high quality feel and appearance.

Standard A partially opened staple fibre with plenty of bounce and bulk.

I like to use the best quality for all my projects whether large or small, and although this filling is the most expensive it has very high bulk and so it goes a lot further than cheaper fillings. However, any of the man-made fibre types are preferable to kapok which is messy to work with and cannot be washed, or foam chips which are dangerous.

Some of the toys are partly filled with beans to make bean bags and commercially made plastic granules are now available which conform to British safety standards (see list of stockists). You can of course substitute dried lentils or rice, but the toy would not be washable.

Fur Fabric

You should be able to obtain the fur fabrics used throughout the book quite easily. 'Care Bears' type of fur fabric is mentioned for several of the toys and this has a very short pile, with a polished surface. When 'fur fabric' itself is quoted, this is the regular type with short pile. 'Polished fur fabric' is the same type but with a polished surface.

Knitting yarn

When double-knitting yarn is mentioned, USA readers should use knitting worsted weight; Australian readers should use 8 ply.

Velcro hook and loop fastener

This is sold by the centimetre or inch and is available from fabric shops and haberdashery departments in a variety of colours.

Velcro is composed of two flat narrow nylon strips, one strip has hundreds of tiny hooks and the other has a furry surface composed of minute loops. When the strips are pressed firmly together the hooks catch in the loops and the strip cannot be pulled apart sideways. However, they can be separated simply by peeling them apart.

Iron-on interfacing

Sometimes called interlining, this non-woven type of fabric is used in dressmaking to add firmness or stiffening to collars and facings. It is bonded onto the wrong side of the fabric by ironing. Interfacing is sold by the metre or yard and is available from dress-fabric shops in light, medium and firm weights. There are two colours only, white for light coloured fabrics and charcoal grey for darker shades.

GENERAL INSTRUCTIONS

Measurements

All sizes are given in metric, with the imperial measurements in brackets. During the designing process I work out each measurement individually, to suit both metric and imperial, and you will notice that sets of measurements do not always convert in exactly the same way. I often round them off to avoid an awkward size, for example a straight strip of fabric 13cm in length should convert accurately to 5⅛in. If the ⅛in will make no difference whatsoever to the finished item, then it is rounded down to 5in. All such inconsistencies are deliberate and not printing errors. Simply stick to metric or imperial throughout each design, whichever you prefer.

Copying the patterns

For tracing the patterns off the page, use ordinary plain white paper such as that used in inexpensive jotting pads, or the cheapest typing paper. Just make sure that the pattern outlines are visible through the paper. I always use typing paper for my patterns and they withstand repeated use. When they get a bit holey from constant pinning, they can be repaired with bits of sticky tape.

Tracing paper is not really suitable for patterns as it is too crisp to be pinned many times without tearing. To trace the patterns off the page, first fix the paper securely to the page with tiny bits of reusable adhesive putty, such as Sticky Tack or Blue Tack. Trace off the outlines. Mark all details onto the pattern pieces, then remove the paper from the page and cut out the patterns. Some patterns have to be traced onto folded paper because you will only be able to get a perfectly symmetrical shape this way. You should do this as follows:

Fold a piece of paper in half, making sure that it is large enough for both halves to cover the complete area of the pattern. Crease the fold sharply. Now open up the folded paper, having the outer sharp edge of fold uppermost. Flatten the fold.

Place this folded edge along the line indicated on the pattern, then secure paper to page with bits of putty. Trace off the pattern outline onto the paper. Remove the paper from the page and refold it, making sure your pattern outline is on the outside.

You now have to cut out the pattern through both thicknesses and this can be a bit tricky as the two paper layers tend to slip apart as you cut, especially if the pattern is a large one. To counteract this, open up the folded paper slightly and put dots of glue on the inside, just outside the area of the pattern outline. The drawn line is easy to see if you hold it up to a strong light.

Now press the paper layers together and they will stay together as you cut out the pattern. Unfold the paper and you have the complete pattern. Some of the pattern pieces are too large to fit onto one page and these are given in two pieces. Special instructions are given for tracing these off when this occurs. Patterns for the larger toys are given scaled down on grids. For drawing out such patterns to full size, you can buy packets of dressmaker's graph paper from dress-fabric shops or haberdashery departments. The paper will be ruled into 5cm squares or 2in squares, according to whether it is metric or imperial. There will also probably be lines ruled between these larger squares – at 1cm intervals (metric) and ¼in intervals (imperial).

If the diagram for the patterns states that each square = 5cm (2in), draw your patterns onto the dressmaker's graph paper accordingly. If the diagram states that each square = 2cm (¾in) or any other measurement you will need to overrule the graph paper into these sizes of squares before drawing out the patterns. Draw the pattern shapes onto the graph paper, following the outline shapes in each square from the diagram.

For circular patterns the measurement given is usually the diameter (the distance across the centre) of the circle. When drawing circles set your compasses to the radius measurement, ie half the diameter. To draw circles which are larger than your compasses can make, take a length of thin string and knot one end around a pencil point. Now tie a knot in the string, the required radius measure-

ment away from the pencil point, keeping the string taut as you measure. Now draw the circle as shown in Diagram 1.

When measurements for simple shapes are given in the instructions (such as squares,

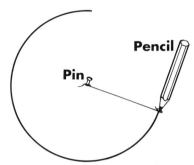

DIAGRAM 1 How to draw large circles using pencil, a pin and a length of string

rectangles or triangles), you can draw these directly on to the wrong side of the fabric before cutting out. However, if the toy is to be made more than once, it is a good idea to cut paper patterns for such shapes and mark on all the details for future use.

Working with fur fabric
On fur fabric, the fur pile lies smooth and flat if stroked in one direction and will lift up if stroked in the opposite direction. On patterns for fur fabric toys, the direction of the 'smooth stroke' of the fur pile is indicated by an arrow on each pattern piece. Always take care to cut out the pieces so that the smooth stroke of the fur pile follows the direction of the arrows and straight grain of the fabric.

To cut out fur fabric pieces, pin the patterns, one at a time, to the wrong side of the fabric then snip through the back of the fabric only, so as not to cut through the fur pile on the right side. When cutting a pair of pieces, always take care to remember to reverse the pattern before cutting the second piece.

To join fur fabric pieces, place the pieces right sides together, tucking in the fur pile at the raw edges, then push in pins at right angles to the raw edges all round, as shown in Diagram 2. After sewing, remove all the pins, then turn right side out and pick out the fur pile trapped in the seam with the point of a pin.

DIAGRAM 2 Holding fur fabric pieces together with pins before sewing seams

Working with felt

Because felt is a non-woven fabric, it is often supposed that it has no grain. However, it does have varying amounts of stretch when pulled lengthways and sideways and usually stretches most across the width, that is from selvedge to selvedge. When using felt for stuffed toys, always cut any identical pieces so that they lie in the same direction, parallel with the selvedge, or a straight edge if a square of felt is being used.

Diagram 3(A) shows an example of the correct way to cut the pieces for a doll's feet. If the feet are cut as shown in Diagram 3(B) there may be differences in size after stuffing

A (Right way)

B (Wrong way)

DIAGRAM 3 Cutting out felt pieces

due to the felt stretching more in one direction than the other.

If the most stretch of the felt is marked by arrows on the pattern pieces, be sure to cut out the pieces of felt accordingly, as described.

Felt is used for the facial features on many of the dolls and animals. When cutting out these small felt shapes, the cut edges tend to be rather untidy, because the felt fibres fray out at the cut edges. To counteract this, first spread one surface of the felt with adhesive, work it into the felt with a fingertip, then leave to dry. Take care not to use too much glue, or it will soak through to the other side of the felt. When the glue is dry, place an old cloth on your ironing board to protect it, then press the right side of the felt with a steam iron or hot iron over a damp cloth. When you cut the pieces from felt treated in this way, the cut edges will be much smoother. This method should not be used on felt pieces which are to be stitched and stuffed, of course.

To neaten cut edges of trimmings

Spread a little adhesive on the wrong side of any braid or trimmings, at the position where it is to be cut. Leave to dry before cutting. If adding a ribbon bow to a design, leave the ends a little longer than necessary and spread the back of the ribbon ends with a little glue before cutting to the required length.

Ordinary shoe-lace and sports shoe-lace can be sealed in the same way. These laces are usually tubular in construction so you can open the ends by pushing in a pencil point, dot a little glue inside, then press the raw edges together. When the glue is dry, trim off the ragged ends.

Making rag dolls (woven fabric)

Any fine, closely woven calico, cotton or poly/cotton fabric is suitable for doll-making. While pink and peachy shades look best, cream or white can also be used. Pale pink is sometimes difficult to get in a dress fabric, but may be obtainable as sheeting. Many shops now have sheeting by the metre (or yard) for making duvet covers etc. If you do a lot of doll-making it is worth looking out for sale or bargain offers of sheets in the larger chain stores. A sheet bought in this way can work out cheaper than buying fabric by the metre or yard.

Always cut out the doll pieces on the straight grain of the fabric unless the pattern indicates otherwise. There is a certain amount of stretch in woven cotton fabrics across the width from selvedge to selvedge, while the lengthways grain of the fabric does not stretch at all. If there are arrows on the pattern pieces indicating the *width,* take care to cut out the pieces accordingly. The toy has been designed to make use of this stretch in the fabric.

When joining the doll pieces, use a small machine stitch, and trim seams around all the curved edges leaving about 3mm (⅛in). After stuffing, any puckers in the seams can be ironed out as follows. Pinch the toy tightly between finger and thumb to force the stuffing against the puckered seam, then rub the seam against a warm iron.

Making rag dolls (stockinette)

Cotton stockinette, in flesh or cream colour, is available by the metre or yard specifically for making dolls. Alternatively, discarded plain white stockinette vests or T-shirts can be used instead. These can be tinted pink if desired, following the dye-maker's instructions. When dyeing fabric remember that the colour always looks darker when the fabric is wet. Test a small cutting in the dye solution first.

Although stockinette will stretch in any direction when pulled, it usually stretches most across the width, as in hand-knitted fabric. The direction of 'most stretch' is indicated by arrows on each pattern piece, or in the instructions when making dolls from stockinette.

Use a small machine stitch when sewing stockinette, stretching the seams slightly as you stitch, so that the threads will not snap when the pieces are stuffed. Trim the seams around all the curves leaving about 3mm (⅛in).

Seams

Seams and turnings are allowed on all the pattern pieces, the allowances being stated in each set of instructions.

Join the fabric pieces with *right sides* together unless otherwise stated. If you are joining two very large pieces together, first mark your pattern with short lines at regular intervals round the edges and mark these onto the wrong side of the fabric before removing the pattern and after cutting out the pieces. They can then be joined accurately together, matching the marks all round.

To mark dart lines onto the fabric, push a pencil point through the pattern and into the fabric at intervals along the lines, then join up the dots after removing the pattern. Mark any dots on the patterns with pencil point in the same way.

'Trim seams' in the instructions means to trim away *half* of the seam allowance. When making items of clothing, press all the seams open after they are stitched, unless other instructions are given.

Stuffing the toy

Lumpy toys are usually the result of uneven stuffing, because small gaps are left where one piece of filling ends and the next begins. This happens most frequently in narrow pieces such as the limbs of a rag doll. When stuffing these, take a large handful of filling (polyester, not kapok which falls apart) and tease it into an elongated shape. Push one end of the filling into the end of the limb, then gradually feed in the filling with the fingers, trying to keep it in a continuous piece. Keep feeling the limb as it is stuffed, both inside and outside, taking care to fill any empty areas. When the piece of filling is almost finished, introduce one end of another piece in the same way, so the fibres of the first piece blend with the next.

If the limb is too narrow to get a finger inside, push in filling with the end of a pencil or knob of a knitting needle. To stuff very small toys, use tweezers.

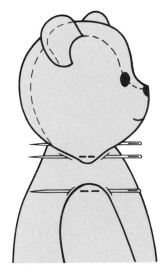

DIAGRAM 4 Use darning needles to hold the head or limb to the body before sewing in place

Attaching a head or limb

To hold the head or limb of a toy securely to the body while sewing it in place, use darning needles instead of pins. Push the needles first into the body fabric, then into the head or limb, then back into the body fabric as shown in Diagram 4.

Ladder stitch

This stitch is used for closing the opening on a soft toy after stuffing. The raw edges of the fabric are turned in at the seam line, then the folded edges are 'laced' together from side to side forming stitches which look like a ladder. Use strong double thread and take small, straight stitches alternately along one side then the other. After working a few stitches, pull the thread up tight, thus bringing the fabric edges together (see Diagram 5). Ladder stitch can also be used to make an invisible joint when attaching the head or limb of a toy to the body.

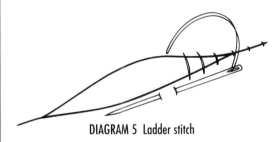

DIAGRAM 5 Ladder stitch

Safety-lock eyes

For some of the toys, plastic safety eyes are used – these are fixed securely in place with press-on washers on the inside. Once fixed, the eyes are almost impossible to remove, so mark the eye positions very accurately. Take care not to put the washers on the eye shanks until they are actually being fixed in place. (If you do need to remove the eyes, the plastic shanks can be snipped or sawn off close to the washers, then you should be able to prise off the washers.) To insert the eyes, make a tiny hole with point of scissors at each eye dot. Widen the holes by pushing a knitting needle through from the right side of the fabric. Push the shank of the eye through one hole to the wrong side of fabric. Place the eye on a flat surface and position the washer on the end of the eye shank, with curved-up prongs of the washer uppermost. Now using your thumbs, push the washer very firmly down the shank as far as it will go. Repeat

with the other eye. Test that the eyes are properly fixed – you should not be able to get your fingernails between the eye and the washer.

Making a face

The age and character of a doll or toy are mainly determined by the positioning of the facial features. For a child-like appearance the eyes should be placed half-way down the face. If they are too close together the face will look mean, too far apart and the eyes will be frog-like. Therefore if measurements are given in the instructions for placing facial features, always follow these and your toy should look exactly like the one in the illustration.

If the eyes are made from felt, first pin them to the face, pushing the pins straight through the eyes and into the toy. Now check that they are level and centrally placed on the face by looking at the toy in a mirror. Any irregularities will show up immediately. The same method can be used if eyes and noses are to be embroidered, by pinning small paper shapes to the face before actually marking the fabric. An embroidered mouth line can be marked in the same way using a short length of thick thread or yarn pinned to the face as a guide.

When embroidering facial features, secure the knotted end of the thread in a place where it will not be seen on the finished toy – for example, at the back of a doll's head or under the position of a felt eye or nose on an animal. Use a long darning needle to take the thread through the toy to the position of the embroidered feature. Work the feature using a small sewing needle, then use the darning needle to take the thread back through the toy as before and fasten off the thread.

When sewing or glueing felt features on a fur fabric toy, snip away the fur pile beneath the felt before fixing it in place.

Colouring cheeks

Use an orange-red pencil for colouring a doll's cheeks and always try the effect on an oddment of fabric first. Gently rub the side of the pencil tip (not the point) over the cheek area. If the colour is too strong or uneven, some of it may be removed by rubbing gently with a soft eraser.

Two Tubby Teddies

Printed cotton fabric is used for the bodies, arms and legs of these teddies so that very little fur fabric is required and they are quite economical to make. Each one measures 38cm (15in) from the ears to the feet. The skirt and the pants can be removed for extra play value.

You will need: 30cm (⅜yd) of 138cm (54in) wide Care Bears type short pile fawn fur fabric (enough to make the two teddies); 350g (12oz) stuffing for each teddy; scraps of black felt; strong thread for gathering by hand; adhesive.

In addition you will need:

For girl teddy: 45cm (½yd) of 91cm (36in) wide printed cotton fabric; 1.80m (2yd) of lace edging; 1.40m (1½yd) of broderie anglaise edging about 3cm (1⅛in) in width; 60cm (24in) length of narrow ribbon; small strip of Velcro hook-and-loop fastener.

For boy teddy: 45cm (½yd) of 91cm (36in) wide printed cotton fabric; 1.30m (1½yd) of lace edging; a 37cm (14½in) length of 1.5cm (⅝in) wide elastic; 60cm (24in) length of ribbon.

Notes: For the teddy head gusset pattern, trace the pattern onto folded paper as indicated, then cut out and open up to give full-sized pattern. Trace all other patterns off the page and mark on details.

5mm (¼in) seams are allowed on all pieces unless otherwise stated. Take care to have smooth stroke of fur pile in directions shown on patterns.

BASIC TEDDY

Make all the pieces before assembling.

Head

Cut one gusset and one pair of head pieces from fur fabric. Mark positions of ear and eye dots on the gusset with threads taken from wrong side to right side of fabric. Join head pieces at centre front edges. Sew the side edges of the gusset to head pieces from centre front matching points A, over top of head to back neck edge matching points B. Turn head right side out and stuff firmly, pushing stuffing firmly into snout also. Run a strong gathering thread round the neck edge, pull up tightly to close and fasten off.

Cut four ear pieces from fur fabric. Oversew them together in pairs leaving lower edges open. Turn right side out then oversew lower edges together pulling stitches to gather slightly. Sew ears to sides of head starting at the marking threads on the gusset.

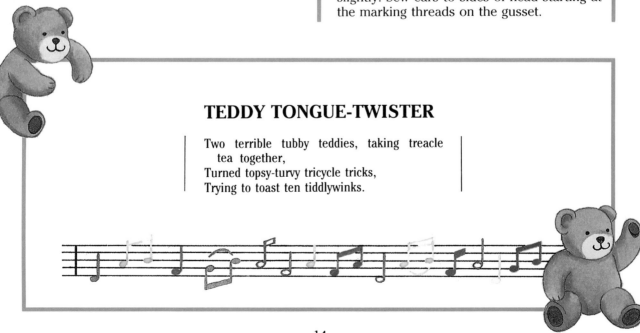

TEDDY TONGUE-TWISTER

Two terrible tubby teddies, taking treacle tea together,
Turned topsy-turvy tricycle tricks,
Trying to toast ten tiddlywinks.

Cut eyes from black felt and work a highlight on each one with white thread. Trim off fur pile around the threads marking the centre of each eye. Glue eyes in place. Cut nose from two layers of black felt glued together. Glue, then sew it to end of snout.

Body

Cut two pairs of body pieces from printed fabric. Mark leg dots on wrong side of each piece. Work running threads to join up the dots so that the stitches show on the right side of fabric. Join body pieces in pairs at centre edges. Join these pairs all round outer edges leaving the neck edges open. Turn right side out and stuff firmly. Use strong thread to

gather round neck edge, pull up gathers and continue stuffing to fill firmly, then pull up gathers tightly to close and fasten off.

Legs

Cut two pairs of foot pieces and two soles from fur fabric. Join the foot pieces in pairs at centre front edges. Cut two leg pieces from printed fabric and mark positions of dots shown on the pattern with threads on right side of fabric. Gather the ankle edge of each leg piece to fit the ankle edge of each foot, then sew in place with right sides together and raw edges level. Join centre back edges of feet and legs. Pin, then oversew soles to lower edges of feet matching centre front and centre back points. Machine-stitch through the oversewn edges to reinforce the seam. Turn down 1cm (⅜in) at top raw edges of legs and tack. Turn legs right side out and stuff. Sew lace edging round lower edge of each leg piece.

Arms

Cut four hand pieces from fur fabric and join them in pairs at one side as shown on the pattern. For each arm cut a 12x20cm (4¾x8in) strip of printed fabric. Gather one long edge of each strip to fit wrist edge of each hand then stitch in place with right sides together and raw edges level. Now join remainder of hand seam and also short edges of arms. Turn right side out and stuff hands, then stuff arms more lightly. Sew lace edging round wrists to match legs.

To assemble

Place the head on top of the body, matching the gathers and also centre fronts and backs. Use strong thread to ladder-stitch head and body together working round a few times to secure.

Pin open top edges of the legs to lower edge of body just outside the lines of marking threads, matching the threads at dots on legs to the outer seam on the body. Slip-stitch the legs in place, adding more stuffing to fill and make firm before completing sewing.

Sew the gathered tops of the arms to sides of body 2.5cm (1in) below the neck. Sew the arms to body seam also, about 3cm (1⅛in) below the gathered tops.

GIRL TEDDY

Make the basic teddy, then tie ribbon in a bow round neck.

Skirt

Cut a 13×91cm (5×36in) strip of printed fabric. Narrowly hem one long edge. Gather the raw edge of the broderie anglaise trimming to fit this hemmed edge, then sew it to the wrong side of hem. Sew lace edging to right side of skirt above the hem. Join short edges of the skirt taking a 1cm (⅜in) seam and leaving 5cm (2in) open at top waist edge. Press the seam to one side and neaten the raw edges. Gather the raw waist edge to measure 38cm (15in). Bind with a 4×39cm (1½×15½in) strip of printed fabric for the waistband. Sew Velcro to the ends of the waistband.

BOY TEDDY

Make the basic teddy, then tie ribbon in a bow round neck.

Pants

Cut two pants pieces from printed fabric. Narrowly hem the ankle edges and sew on lace edging. Join the pieces at the centre edges then clip seams at curves.

Bring the centre seams together and join the inside leg edges of each leg. Turn down the waist edge 5mm (¼in), then 2cm (¾in) and press. Turn pants right side out. Join ends of the length of elastic. Stitch down the waist edge of pants enclosing the elastic as you go.

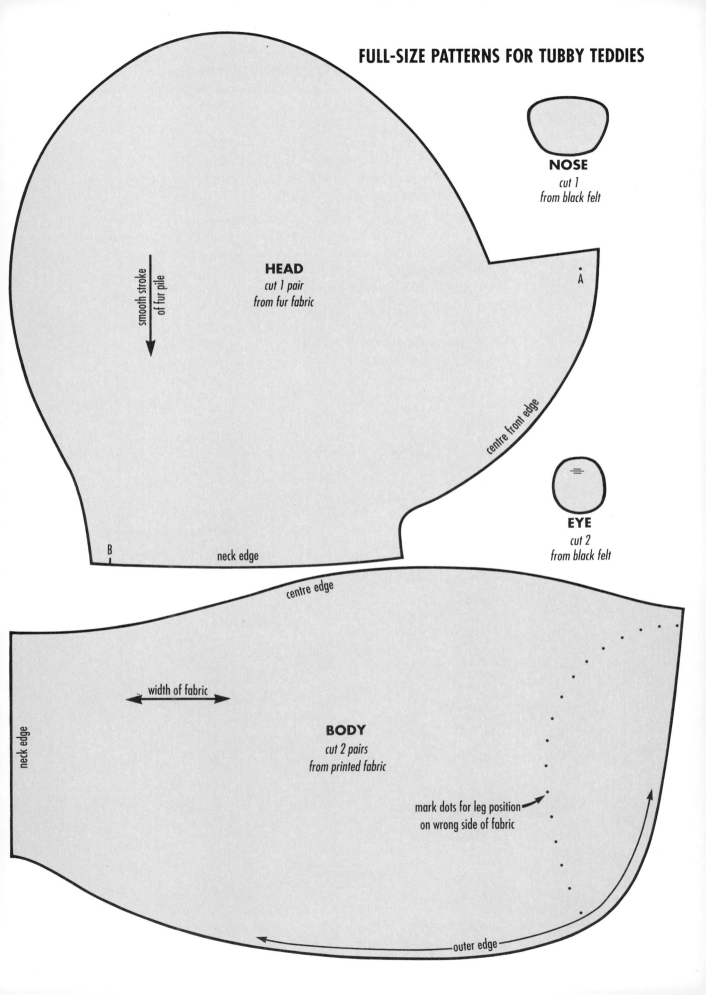

FULL-SIZE PATTERNS FOR TUBBY TEDDIES

NOSE
*cut 1
from black felt*

HEAD
*cut 1 pair
from fur fabric*

smooth stroke
of fur pile

centre front edge

A

B

neck edge

EYE
*cut 2
from black felt*

centre edge

width of fabric

neck edge

BODY
*cut 2 pairs
from printed fabric*

mark dots for leg position
on wrong side of fabric

outer edge

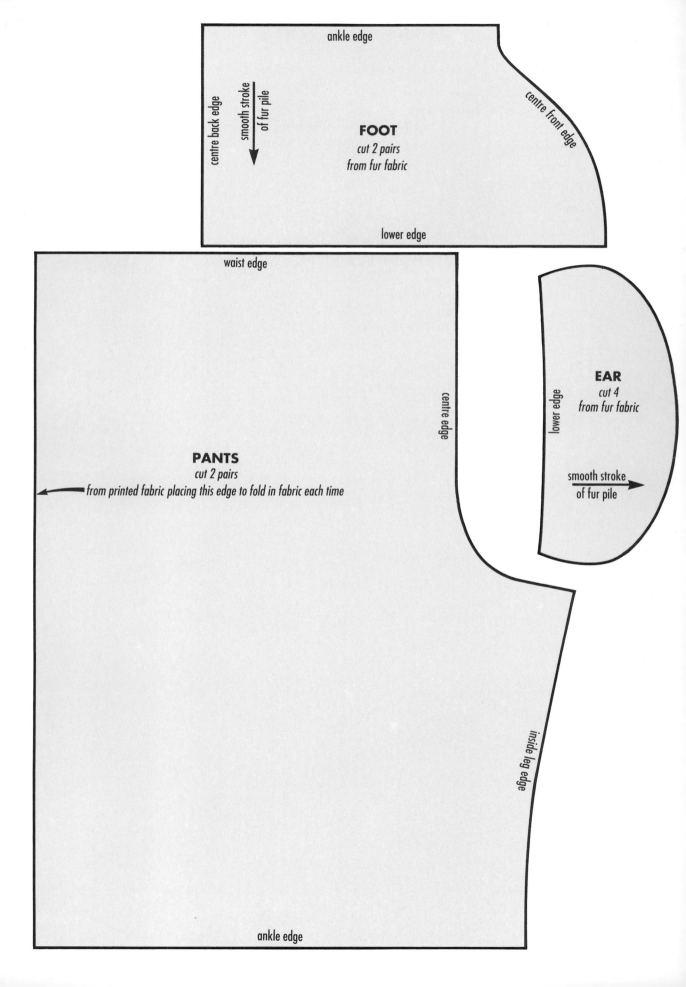

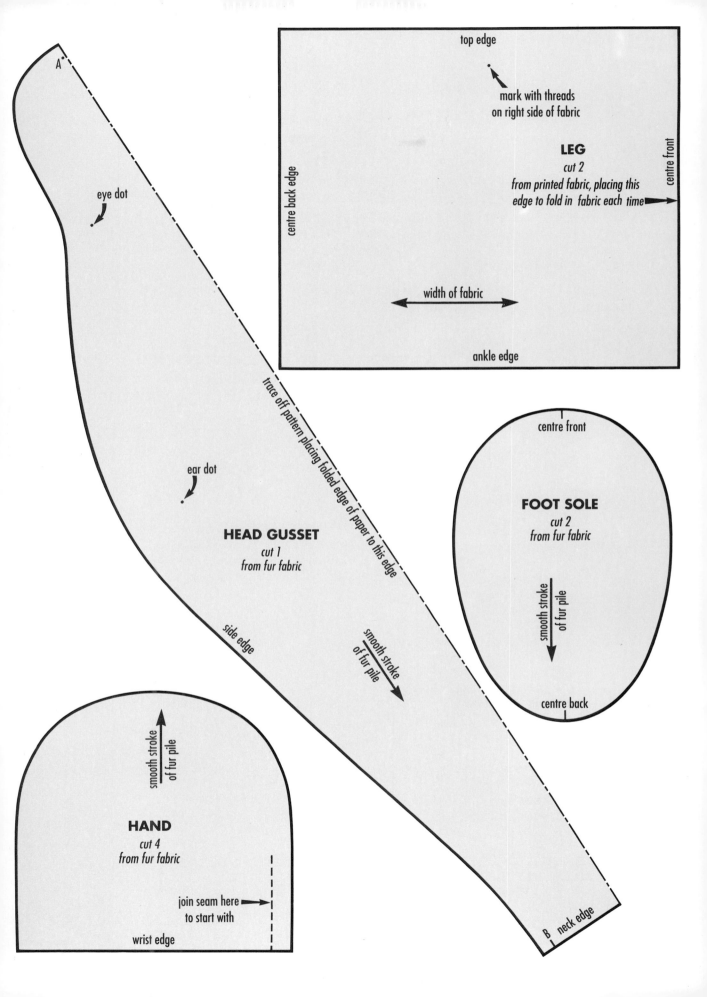

LEG
cut 2
from printed fabric, placing this edge to fold in fabric each time

top edge

mark with threads
on right side of fabric

centre back edge

centre front

width of fabric

ankle edge

A

eye dot

ear dot

trace off pattern placing folded edge of paper to this edge

HEAD GUSSET
cut 1
from fur fabric

side edge

smooth stroke
of fur pile

B   neck edge

centre front

FOOT SOLE
cut 2
from fur fabric

smooth stroke
of fur pile

centre back

smooth stroke
of fur pile

HAND
cut 4
from fur fabric

join seam here
to start with

wrist edge

The Camels

Stitch a pair of super-sized cuddly toys which are very easy to make from the same basic shapes. Father camel (large enough for a child to sit on) is 61cm (24in) high and about 61cm (24in) long, not counting his front legs and tail. Baby camel is 35cm (14in) high and the same in length, just right for a cuddly toy.

THE LARGE CAMEL

You will need: 1.60m (1¾yd) of 138cm (54in) wide fawn fur fabric; 5kg (11lb) of stuffing; an oddment of light brown fur fabric for eyelids and end of tail (if not available, use fawn fur fabric); an oddment of fawn fabric

THE CAMEL

The camel is an oddity,
A curious sort of chap,
Who can't repair a leaky roof
Or anything like that.

He couldn't join the mounted police,
Or knit, or go to sea,
Or hop-scotch on the way to school,
Or visit friends for tea.

He isn't good at boiling eggs,
Or gardening, or sums,
He finds it hard to read his letters
When the postman comes.

He almost trained a group of fleas,
Creating quite a stir,
But after jumping through the hoop
They got lost in his fur.

When someone taught him crochet work
It wasn't a success,
He started with a woolly scarf
But made a ballroom dress.

He tried to run the marathon
And failed to get the knack of it,
His front legs set off forwards
While his back legs galloped back a bit.

Last June he travelled Way Out West
With boots and spurs that rattled,
But couldn't croon a cowboy toon
While roundin' up the cattle.

He ventured up the Matterhorn
But got stuck on a ledge,
The rescue team were so annoyed
They sent him down by sledge.

The camel is an oddity,
And though he isn't smart,
He needs a little loving
And a chance to win your heart.

He isn't good at doing things
Which just confuse and muddle him,
But he will be your faithful pal
You only have to CUDDLE HIM!

or felt for the foot pads and ear linings; scraps of white, black and brown felt and a 16cm (6¼in) length of black boot lace for facial features; a 20g ball of red double-knitting yarn; dressmaker's graph paper (marked in squares according to requirements); adhesive, suitable for sticking fabric without marking it.

Notes: Patterns for facial features are given full size for tracing off the page. For the other patterns draw the shapes onto graph paper, following the outlines on the diagram square by square. Each square on the diagram = 5cm (2in). Mark all details onto each pattern piece.

Cut out all pieces from fabrics as stated on patterns having the smooth stroke of fur fabric pieces in direction shown by arrows on patterns. Note that tail piece is cut on the *bias*.

5mm (¼in) seams are allowed on all pieces unless otherwise stated. After drawing and cutting out the body pattern, mark on the face dart lines, point A and position of tail.

To make

Join the side edges of tail piece and turn right side out. Tack upper edges together and stitch to back of one body piece at marked position, having raw edges level and tail pointing inwards and downwards.

Stitch face darts on each body piece. Now join body pieces round edges, leaving lower edges open. Reinforce seam at the hump and centre back curve by stitching again.

Join the leg pieces in pairs at centre front and back edges. Tack a foot pad to lower edge of each leg, matching centre front and back points. Stitch as tacked. Turn legs right side out and stuff lower halves firmly, then upper portions more lightly. Now push stuffing well

down, bring front and back seams together and put a pin through them to hold pushed-down stuffing in place. Tack upper raw edges of each leg together.

Join the base pieces at centre edges taking a 1cm (⅜in) seam and leaving a 20cm (8in) gap at middle of seam for turning and stuffing. Tack, then stitch top of each leg to positions shown on base, having raw edges of base and legs level. Take care also to have feet pointing upwards, away from base.

Now tack outer edge of base to lower edge of body taking a 1cm (⅜in) seam, matching centres front and centres back, points A and leg markings on body pieces. Stitch seam as tacked. If you find this seam awkward to machine-stitch because of the bulk of the legs inside the body, then use doubled strong thread and back-stitch it by hand instead.

Turn camel right side out and remove pins from legs. Stuff very firmly, beginning with nose, then head and front body, then hump and back of body. Finally stuff centre of body, making this as firm as possible because it is the seating position. Ladder-stitch opening in base using strong thread.

Stuff tail lightly. Join tail end pieces leaving upper edges open. Turn right side out and stuff. Insert lower edge of tail inside upper edge of tail end piece and slip-stitch in place.

Face

Glue two layers of white felt together then cut eyes from this double felt. Oversew round edges. Cut and oversew pupils in the same way, using black felt. Sew pupils to eyes as

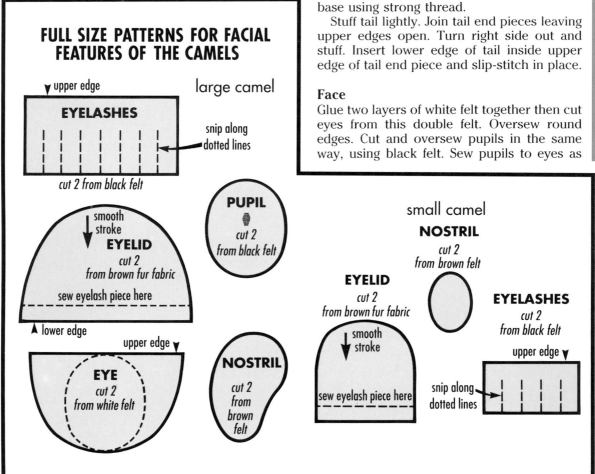

FULL SIZE PATTERNS FOR FACIAL FEATURES OF THE CAMELS

large camel

▼ upper edge

EYELASHES

snip along dotted lines

cut 2 from black felt

smooth stroke

EYELID
cut 2 from brown fur fabric

sew eyelash piece here

▲ lower edge

PUPIL
cut 2 from black felt

EYE
cut 2 from white felt

upper edge ▼

NOSTRIL
cut 2 from brown felt

small camel

NOSTRIL
cut 2 from brown felt

EYELID
cut 2 from brown fur fabric

smooth stroke

sew eyelash piece here

EYELASHES
cut 2 from black felt

upper edge ▼

snip along dotted lines

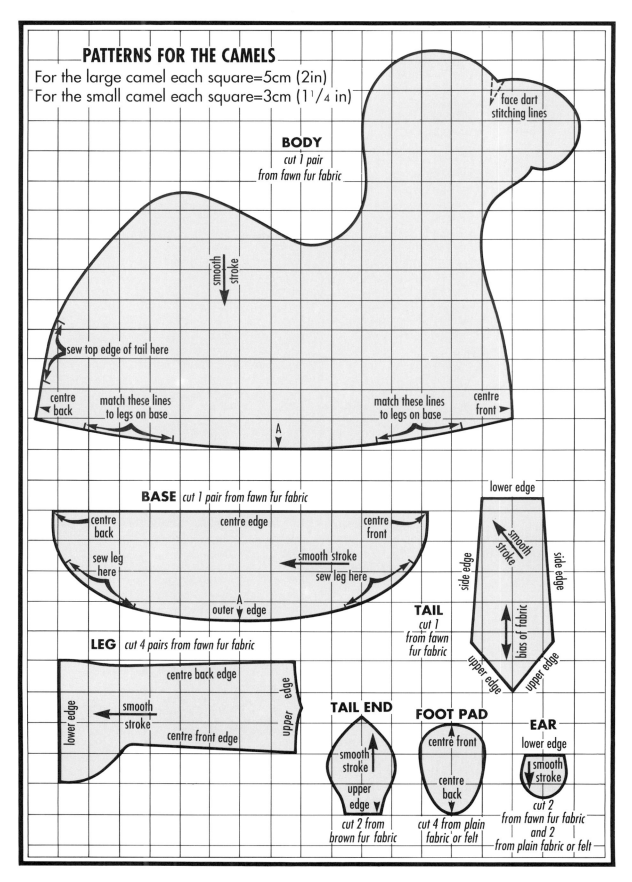

PATTERNS FOR THE CAMELS

For the large camel each square=5cm (2in)
For the small camel each square=3cm (1¹/₄ in)

face dart
stitching lines

BODY
cut 1 pair
from fawn fur fabric

smooth stroke

sew top edge of tail here

centre back
match these lines to legs on base
A
match these lines to legs on base
centre front

BASE *cut 1 pair from fawn fur fabric*

centre back
centre edge
centre front
sew leg here
smooth stroke
sew leg here
outer edge
A

lower edge
smooth stroke
side edge
side edge
bias of fabric
TAIL
cut 1 from fawn fur fabric
upper edge
upper edge

LEG *cut 4 pairs from fawn fur fabric*

centre back edge
upper edge
lower edge
smooth stroke
centre front edge

TAIL END
smooth stroke
upper edge
cut 2 from brown fur fabric

FOOT PAD
centre front
centre back
cut 4 from plain fabric or felt

EAR
lower edge
smooth stroke
cut 2 from fawn fur fabric and 2 from plain fabric or felt

23

shown on the pattern. Use white thread to work a highlight on each pupil as shown on the pattern. Cut two eyelids from fur fabric and trim fur pile short at lower edges. Oversew lower edge of each eyelid to upper edge of each eye, easing edge of eyelid to fit.

For the eyelashes, soak a piece of black felt with the adhesive, pressing it into the felt with the fingertips. Leave to dry then iron the felt, covering it with a piece of thick paper. Cut the eyelash pieces then snip each one as shown on pattern. Trim each eyelash to a point. Pull short ends of eyelash pieces to stretch the upper edge slightly, then sew upper edges to eyelids as shown on eyelid pattern. Sew completed eyes to face placing them 5cm (2in) apart, having lower edges touching the face darts and adding a little stuffing under each eyelid.

Cut nostrils from doubled brown felt and oversew, in the same way as for eye pieces. Sew nostrils to end of face as illustrated. For the mouth, seal the ends of the length of boot lace with adhesive to prevent fraying. Fold the boot lace in half and sew the fold to the face seam about 2.5cm (1in) below nostrils. Pin, then sew boot lace to face forming a shallow W. Trim fur pile above mouth and also above nostrils.

Ears

Join the ear pieces in pairs leaving lower edges open. Turn right side out. Fold in half and oversew all lower raw edges together. Ladder-stitch lower edges of ears to head, placing them 20cm (8in) apart and about 5cm (2in) up from tops of eyelids. Pin ears in upright position and ladder-stitch to head again, to hold in place.

Harness

For the noseband cut twelve 1m (39in) lengths of yarn and knot them together at each end. Loop one knotted end round a door knob, then holding the yarn taut, insert your index finger in the other knotted end. Twist your finger round and round, until when relaxed, the yarn begins to curl tightly back on itself. Bring knotted ends together allowing yarn to curl up evenly along the length. Place this cord round the camel's nose and overlap ends about 2.5cm (1in), then trim off any excess length. Bind the overlapped portion with red yarn to hold it in place, sewing in the end of yarn. Place noseband on the camel's nose with the join placed under the chin.

For remainder of the harness cut twelve 4m (4½yd) lengths of yarn and make a twisted cord in same way as before. Sew centre of this cord to back of camel's head just below ears. Loop each end of the cord round the nose-band level with camel's mouth, then knot ends of cord together and trim off any uneven lengths of yarn.

THE SMALL CAMEL

You will need: 70cm (¾yd) of 138cm (54in) wide fawn fur fabric; 1kg (2lb) of stuffing; an oddment of light brown fur fabric for eyelids and end of tail (if not available use fawn fur fabric); an oddment of fawn fabric or felt for the foot pads and ear linings; scraps of black and brown felt and a 12cm (4¾in) length of black shoe lace for facial features; graph paper and adhesive as for the large camel.
Notes: Instructions as for Large Camel, but over-rule your graph paper at 3cm (1¼in) intervals then draw the patterns, noting that for small camel, each square on the diagram will equal 3cm (1¼in).

To make

Make up exactly as for Large Camel, leaving a 12cm (4¾in) gap in centre seam for turning and stuffing.

Face

Cut nostrils from brown felt and sew them to end of face as illustrated. Trim off fur pile above nostrils. Sew on shoe lace for mouth as for Large Camel, placing folded end about 2.5cm (1in) below nostrils. Trim fur pile above mouth and around chin area. Make eyelashes in the same way as for Large Camel, using pattern given for small camel. Cut eyelids from brown fur fabric and trim off fur pile at lower edges. Sew upper edges of eyelashes to eyelids at position shown on eyelid pattern.

Sew eyelids to face, placing them 3cm (1¼in) apart and having ends of eyelashes touching the face darts.

Ears

Make and sew the ears in place as for Large Camel, having lower edges 8cm (3¼in) apart and about 4cm (1½in) up from tops of eyelids.

Nursery-Tale Teddies

BASIC TEDDY

The basic teddy is 38cm (15in) high and although the toy appears to be 'joined', the joints are in fact sewn. To complete the old-fashioned appearance, plastic safety eyes are inserted. You can dress the teddy in any of the four nursery-tale costumes. All the items of clothing are removable.

For each teddy you will need: 30cm (⅜yd) of 138cm (54in) wide fawn short pile fur fabric (Care Bears type) (50cm [⅝yd] will make a pair of bears); two 12mm (½in) diameter amber safety eyes; 350g (12oz) washable stuffing; scraps of black felt; a length of black double-knitting yarn; strong fawn thread; dressmaker's graph paper marked in 5cm (2in) squares; adhesive.

25

Notes: Copy the pattern pieces off the diagram onto graph paper square by square, each square on the diagram = 5cm (2in). Mark all details on each pattern piece. When cutting out fur-fabric pieces take care to have the smooth stroke of the fur pile following the direction of the arrows on patterns.

5mm (¼in) seams are allowed on all fur-fabric pieces unless otherwise stated.

To make the head

Cut one pair of head pieces. Mark all dots, crosses and lines on wrong side of fabric. Take strands of coloured thread through the mouth dots to the right side of fabric. Mark the ear position lines with a line of fawn back stitches taken through to right side of fabric. Cut out the head gusset and mark on crosses.

Now join head pieces at centre front edges from crosses marked A to the neck edge. Insert gusset over top of head matching crosses marked A and B. Note that because the nose end of gusset is so narrow it is easiest to sew this portion to head by hand, back-stitching securely.

Insert the eyes at the marked positions. Turn head right side out. Stuff firmly, working from back of head towards front, then stuff nose well. Run a strong double gathering thread round neck edge of head and pull up gathers tightly leaving a finger-sized hole, then fasten off. Continue stuffing through the hole to fill area around the gathers.

For mouth, use black yarn and work a straight line from just below point A as far as centre front coloured thread. Next work a straight line to each of the other coloured threads. Fasten off at point A then snip off the coloured threads. Trim fur pile around mouth lines.

Cut nose from three layers of black felt glued together using the full-sized pattern. Oversew round edges of nose. Sew nose in place lapping top edge over end of head gusset. Cut four ear pieces and oversew them together in pairs, leaving lower edges open. Turn right side out and oversew lower edges together, pulling stitches to gather to measure 6cm (2½in). Sew ears securely to marked positions at each side of head. Lay head aside for now.

To make the body and legs

Cut one pair of body pieces. Mark the dots at leg edges then mark and back-stitch the arm sewing lines in same way as for ear lines on head. Join body pieces at centre front and back edges. Bring these seams together and stitch across the short lower edges. Leave body wrong side out.

Cut one pair of inner and one pair of outer leg pieces. Join them in pairs leaving upper edges open. Turn legs right side out. Slip legs inside body so that upper raw edges of legs are level with raw leg edges of body taking care to match arrows on body to centre front and centre back seams on legs and also matching points C. Pin, then oversew the raw edges together. Work round a second time to make seams secure. Turn body right side out. Stuff the legs almost to upper edges then insert pins across the oversewn seams through both thicknesses of fur fabric. Continue stuffing the body firmly, then gather neck edge and finish in same way as for neck edge of head. Remove pins from leg seams. Place head on top of body, matching the finger-sized holes and the centre front seams of both. Ladder-stitch head to body where they touch, working round several times to secure.

To make the arms

Cut two pairs of arm pieces and mark the arms sewing lines on wrong side of each one. Join pieces in pairs leaving seams open above the dots. Turn in the raw edges of these openings and tack down. Turn arms right side out and stuff lower halves. Place an arm at each side of body matching upper edges of arms to lines on body. Pin arm pieces which are nearest to body in place, then sew these to body round upper edges and across the arm sewing lines. Stuff remainder of arms lightly, then sew remaining upper edges of arms in place.

THE OUTFITS

Note: Take 1cm (⅜in) seams, turnings and hems unless otherwise stated.

WEE TEDDY WINKIE

You will need: 45cm (½yd) of 91cm (36in) wide striped fabric; oddment of yarn for tassel; four snap fasteners; four small buttons; 1.50m (1⅝yd) of frilled lace trimming.

Nightshirt

Cut out front, backs and sleeves as stated on the pattern. Join one armhole edge of front to one armhole edge of each sleeve. Repeat with other sleeve. Join armhole edges of backs to remaining armhole edges of sleeves. Trim seams at curves. Join centre back edges of backs from hem, for 7cm (2¾in) only, taking

WEE TEDDY WINKIE

Wee Teddy Winkie runs through the town,
Upstairs and downstairs in his nightgown,
Tapping at the window, crying through the lock,
'Are the Teddies all in bed, for now it's eight o'clock?'

Goodness! It's a wonder that Teddy Winkie didn't get buckets of water chucked all over him for such anti-social behaviour. And no-one really knew why he started all that carry-on, it was quite a mystery. The townsbears got particularly mad on Wednesday evenings when 'Filthy Rich Bears' (a really smashing soap-opera) was on the television.

It got so bad that the bears gathered for a secret meeting in the town hall where they hit on a plan to cure Teddy Winkie of his bad habit. The very next night, as Teddy Winkie was setting off on his rounds, all the townsbears were ready. When he reached the first house, the bear in residence was waiting at the doorstep. 'Here you little nuisance', he said handing Teddy a mop and bucket, 'While you are tapping on my windows you might as well give them a wipe over at the same time – and there's two pence for you if you do a good job.'

Well, Teddy Winkie was so surprised that he couldn't think of a single thing to say. So he set to work and in no time at all the windows were bright and sparkling in the moonlight.

He collected the two pence, skipped off to the next house and was just about to shout through the lock when the door opened and exactly the same thing that had happened before happened all over again. And so it was at every house in town.

By the end of the night Teddy had collected £1.64 and an Irish penny! Of course his nightgown was a bit bedraggled and his paws had gone soggy but otherwise he was ever so pleased with himself.

And now everyone is delighted with Teddy Winkie and his window-cleaning business which is becoming so prosperous that he is thinking of taking on a small apprentice bear.

But I'm afraid that the old nursery rhyme will have to be changed for a new one which goes:

Wee Teddy Winkie runs through the town,
Dressed in something sensible and *not* a nightgown.
He polishes the windows with mop and pail in hand,
And now the townsbears' windows are the cleanest in the land!

Here is Wee Teddy Winkie and his favourite nursery-tale chums: Robear-in-Hood, Cinderbearella and Little Bear Riding Hood. Pictures, patterns and instructions appear on the following pages.

a 2.5cm (1in) seam. Neaten raw edges of seam then press to one side. Hem lower edges of front and back. Join front to back at side edges then join underarm edges of sleeves. Clip underarm edges of these seams. Hem lower edges of sleeves and sew on trimming.

Bind neck edge with a 3x28cm (1¼x11in) bias strip of fabric, taking 5mm (¼in) seams and stretching bias to fit when sewing it on. Sew trimming round neck and down centre front as illustrated, then sew on buttons. Sew snaps to back opening.

Nightcap
Cut two pieces as stated on pattern and join them, leaving lower edges open. Trim seam at

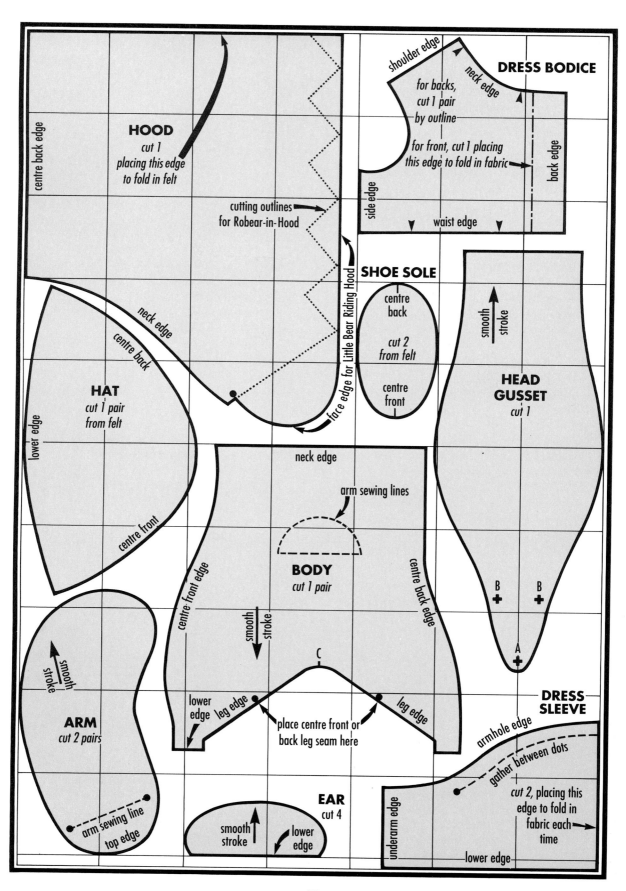

HOOD
cut 1
placing this edge
to fold in felt

centre back edge

cutting outlines
for Robear-in-Hood

DRESS BODICE

shoulder edge

neck edge

for backs,
cut 1 pair
by outline

for front, cut 1 placing
this edge to fold in fabric

back edge

side edge

waist edge

SHOE SOLE

centre
back

cut 2
from felt

centre
front

face edge for Little Bear Riding Hood

neck edge

centre back

HAT
cut 1 pair
from felt

lower edge

centre front

**HEAD
GUSSET**
cut 1

smooth stroke

B   B

A

neck edge

arm sewing lines

BODY
cut 1 pair

centre front edge

smooth stroke

centre back edge

C

lower
edge

leg edge

place centre front or
back leg seam here

leg edge

**DRESS
SLEEVE**

armhole edge

gather between dots

cut 2, placing this
edge to fold in
fabric each
time

ARM
cut 2 pairs

smooth stroke

arm sewing line

top edge

EAR
cut 4

smooth
stroke

lower
edge

underarm edge

lower edge

28

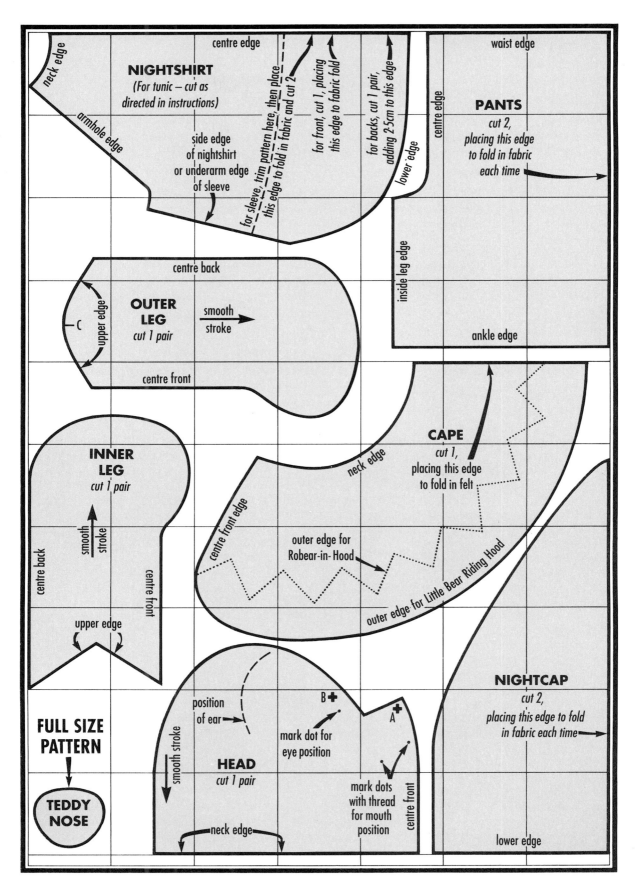

NIGHTSHIRT
(For tunic – cut as directed in instructions)

neck edge

centre edge

armhole edge

side edge of nightshirt or underarm edge of sleeve

for sleeve, trim pattern here, then place this edge to fold in fabric

for front, cut 1, placing this edge to fabric fold

for backs, cut 1 pair, adding 2·5cm to this edge

lower edge

PANTS
cut 2, placing this edge to fold in fabric each time

waist edge

centre edge

inside leg edge

ankle edge

OUTER LEG
cut 1 pair

centre back

upper edge

C

smooth stroke

centre front

INNER LEG
cut 1 pair

smooth stroke

centre back

centre front

upper edge

centre front edge

neck edge

outer edge for Robear-in-Hood

outer edge for Little Bear Riding Hood

CAPE
cut 1, placing this edge to fold in felt

NIGHTCAP
cut 2, placing this edge to fold in fabric each time

lower edge

FULL SIZE PATTERN

position of ear

mark dot for eye position

B

A

mark dots with thread for mouth position

centre front

smooth stroke

HEAD
cut 1 pair

neck edge

TEDDY NOSE

top point. Hem lower edge and sew on trimming. Make a tassel from yarn and sew to top point of cap.

LITTLE BEAR RIDING HOOD

Pants
You will need: 20cm (¼yd) of 91cm (36in) wide fabric; 90cm (1yd) of lace edging; a short length of narrow elastic.

Cut two pants pieces as directed on pattern. Hem ankle edges, cut lace edging in two pieces and gather to fit, then sew in place. Join pants pieces to each other at centre edges. Stitch again at curves then trim seams at curves. Bring centre seams together and join inside leg edges of each leg. Clip seams where centre seams join. Take a 5mm (¼in) then a 1cm (⅜in) turning on waist edge and stitch. Thread elastic through to fit waist.

Dress
You will need: 45cm (½yd) of 91cm (36in) wide printed cotton fabric; 1.20m (1⅜yd) of trimming; three snap fasteners; short lengths of narrow elastic.

Cut bodice front and back pieces as directed on pattern. Join front bodice to backs at shoulder edges. Make bodice lining in same way, from same fabric. Join lining to bodice at back edges and round neck edges. Trim seam and corners, turn right side out and press. Tack armhole and waist edges of lining and bodice together.

Cut two sleeves. Hem lower edges as for waist edge of pants and thread elastic through to fit upper arms, securing elastic at each end with a few stitches. Gather armhole edges of sleeves between dots and pull up gathers to fit armhole edges of bodice. Sew in place, then stitch again close to first stitching line. Trim seams close to second stitching line. Now join side edges of bodice and underarm edges of sleeves.

For the skirt cut a 15x91cm (6x36in) strip of fabric. Sew on trimming 4cm (1½in) away from one long edge (hem edge of skirt). Join short edges from hem edge for 6cm (2¼in) only, taking a 1.5cm (⅝in) seam. Neaten raw edges of seam and press to one side. Hem lower edge of skirt. Gather waist edge of skirt to fit waist edge of bodice and stitch in place. Neaten raw edges of seam. Sew trimming to bodice in a V-point to waist at centre front, then round neck edge. Sew snap fasteners to back edges.

Cape and Hood
You will need: 30cm (⅜yd) of red felt; 1.50m (1⅝yd) of green bias binding; 45cm (½yd) of ribbon for ties.

Cut cape and hood pieces from felt as directed on patterns. Join centre back edges of hood taking a 5mm (¼in) seam. Join neck edge of hood between the dots to neck edge of cape, taking a 5mm (¼in) seam and easing hood to fit cape. Turn the seam up towards hood and stitch flat. Bind outer edges of cape and hood with bias binding. Cut ribbon in two pieces and sew to cape at each neck edge.

CINDERBEARELLA

Pants
Make these as for Little Bear Riding Hood, using fabric and trimming to match the dress.

Dress and head ornaments
You will need: 45cm (½yd) of 91cm (36in) wide taffeta fabric; 2m (2¼yd) of slotted lace trimming (or other trimming of your choice); 3.30m (3⅝yd) of ribbon to slot through the lace; three snap fasteners; rosebuds or guipure flowers.

Trim 5mm (¼in) off the neck edge of bodice pattern. Cut backs and front and make bodice and lining in same way as for Little Bear Riding Hood (page 30). Join lining to bodice round neck and back edges, then round armhole edges. Trim seams and corners, turn right side out and press. Join side edges of bodice then lining and trim the seams.

For the skirt cut a 21x91cm (8¼x36in) strip of fabric. Join short edges for 10cm (4in) only taking a 1.5cm (⅝in) seam. Neaten raw edges and press seam to one side. Hem lower edge of skirt and sew on lace, slotted with ribbon, then add rosebuds at intervals. Gather waist edge of skirt to fit waist edge of bodice then sew in place leaving lining free. Turn in waist edge of lining and slip-stitch it over seam.

Sew ribbon round neck edge of bodice easing it round the curves. Cut a strip of lace to fit over shoulders from centre front waist of bodice to back waist, adding a bit extra for gathering at V-point at front. Thread ribbon through lace then sew in position with small running stitches on either side of ribbon.

Sew three loops of ribbon to the V-point to hang over the skirt. For the rosette, cut a 20cm (8in) strip of lace and fold it off-centre along length. Gather up tightly and join short ends. Sew to front point with a rosebud at the

centre. Sew rosebuds to the lace trimming over shoulders at intervals. Sew snap fasteners to back edges of bodice.

For each head ornament make a rosette and ribbon loops as for the one on bodice. Sew a loop of ribbon to back of each one, just large enough to slip over bear's ear.

Slippers
You will need: 50cm (20in) of silver lurex braid about 3cm (1¼in) in width, scraps of felt; a short length of shirring elastic; adhesive.

Cut braid into two equal lengths. Join short edges of each one taking a narrow seam. Glue the seams to one side. Cut soles from felt and pin braid round edge of sole matching braid seam to centre back of sole. Tack close to edges easing braid to fit, then stitch as tacked. Turn right side out, and thread elastic through top of shoe, knotting ends at back, to fit bear's feet. Glue down cut ends of elastic.

ROBEAR-IN-HOOD

Pants
Make these as for Little Bear Riding Hood, but use ric-rac sewn to hemmed lower edges instead of lace edging.

Tunic
You will need: 20cm (¼yd) of 91cm (36in) wide felt; 1.40m (1⅝yd) of ric-rac braid.

Use the nightshirt pattern for the tunic. Shorten the pattern by trimming off lower edge 2cm (¾in) below the sleeve trimming line. For back, cut one piece, placing centre edge to fold in felt. For fronts cut one pair by the outline then round off top corners at centre edges.

Next trim 2cm (¾in) off lower edge of your tunic pattern and cut two sleeves, placing centre edge of pattern to fold in felt each time. Join armhole edges of pieces as for nightshirt then trim seams close to the stitching lines. Turn in and catch down lower edges of sleeves then sew on ric-rac. Join fronts to back at side edges then join under-arm edges of sleeves. Trim seams close to stitching. Turn in all remaining outer edges of tunic and catch down, then sew on ric-rac.

Cape and Hood and Hat
You will need: 30cm (⅜yd) of green felt; 45cm (½yd) of cord for the ties; 40cm (16in) of ric-rac braid and a feather, for trimming hat.

Make as for Little Bear Riding Hood but cut outer edges of both pattern pieces by the dotted V-shaped outlines shown. Using contrasting thread, stitch about 5mm (¼in) away from edges of cape and hood.

Cut one pair of hat pieces and join them, taking a 5mm (¼in) seam and leaving the lower edges open. Trim seam and turn right side out. For band round lower edge of hat cut a 4x36cm (1½x14¼in) strip of felt. Join short edges taking narrow seam. Join one long edge to lower edge of hat having right side of band to wrong side of hat and taking a narrow seam. Turn this seam towards hat and stitch it down. Hem other long edge of band and sew on ric-rac. Turn up band. Sew feather to one side.

Belt
You will need: a small buckle with centre prong removed; 45cm (18in) length of firm ribbon to suit width of buckle; a snap fastener.

Stitch all round edge of ribbon with contrast thread, attach one end to buckle. Sew on snap fastener to hold end of belt in position when fastened on teddy.

Isabella

Isabella is a beautiful 61cm (24in) rag doll with a complete outfit of removable clothes – pantaloons, petticoat and lace-trimmed dress and hat. She is sure to be a favourite with every little girl.

THE DOLL

For the doll you will need: 60cm (¾yd) of 91cm (36in) wide pink or white cotton fabric; 500g (18oz) of stuffing; two 20g (¾oz) balls of double-knitting yarn and a 10cm (4in) length of white tape for the hair; for the shoes – small pieces of felt, strong rigid card, ribbon, braid and two small buttons; a scrap of dark brown felt for the eyes; red pencil; adhesive.

Patterns for doll and clothes: Trace all the patterns off the pages onto thin paper, then mark on all the details. Note that some patterns have had to be printed on two pages because they are too large for one page. After tracing, join these at the dotted lines X–Y.

Notes: Cut out all the doll pieces having the width of the fabric (ie selvedge to selvedge) running in the direction shown by the arrows on pattern pieces.

5mm (¼in) seams are allowed unless otherwise stated. Stuff firmly. When stuffing arms and legs where it is difficult to reach lowest parts, roll the leg or arm fabric back on itself, then gradually roll upwards as you stuff.

To make the body and head
Cut one pair of pieces for the back by the pattern outline. Cut one piece for the front, placing the dotted edge indicated on pattern

MEASLES

It's horrible having the measles,
Your friends cannot come round to tea,
But I won't shed a tear,
'Cause my dolly is here,
And dollies can't catch them you see!

to fold in fabric. On the wrong side of each piece lightly mark the neck fold and dart lines. On the wrong side of the front piece lightly mark the mouth line and the leg sewing line. On wrong side of both pieces mark the arm stitching lines. Run coloured tacking threads along the leg sewing line and the arm stitching lines, so they can be seen on right side of the fabric. Now machine-stitch four times along the mouth line on wrong side of fabric using red thread. Draw thread ends to wrong side and knot, then trim off.

Join the back pieces at centre back edges taking a 1cm (⅜in) seam and leaving a gap in seam as shown on pattern. Press seam open and tack down raw edges of opening. Fold the back and the front pieces at the neck fold lines and stitch along dart lines as marked. Trim fabric at each fold line. Join front to back all round edges. Trim seam. Turn right side out and stuff head, pushing stuffing in firmly at sides of face then at neck. Stuff the body, then ladder-stitch the gap in back seam.

Soften the mouth line by shading lightly with red pencil over the stitching then shade a small line at each corner. For the nose, shade a small round area 2.5cm (1in) above the mouth. Cut the eyes from brown felt and work a small highlight on each one with white thread as shown on the pattern. Glue the eyes in place, with lower edges level with upper edge of nose and leaving a 3cm (1⅛in) space between them. Colour cheeks with red pencil.

Hair

For the fringe, sew a few 8cm (3in) long loops of yarn to centre top seam of head then sew them to the face 2cm (¾in) below the head seam. To cover the back of the head cut about twenty 1.30m (52in) lengths of yarn. Back-stitch one lot of ends of the yarn strands to one side of the doll's face as shown on the pattern. Take the strands across the back of the head then sew them to the face at the opposite side in the same way as before. Repeat this, taking strands back and forth, working towards the top of the head until the back of the head is covered. Trim off any excess length. Now back-stitch all the strands to the head at centre-back seam line.

For the front portion of hair, cut the remaining yarn into 65cm (26in) lengths and stitch the centres of strands to the strip of tape, leaving 1cm (⅜in) of tape uncovered at each end. Turn in the ends of tape and pin to centre parting of head beginning at point A shown on the pattern and having tape against head. Back-stitch to the head through stitch-

ing line on the tape. Bring the strands together at each side of the head, just in front of the position of lowest strands of the back hair. Tie the strands together and catch to the head at this position. Trim ends of hair evenly.

Arms

Cut two pairs of arm pieces and join them, leaving upper edges open. Trim seams. Turn and stuff to within 5cm (2in) of the upper edges. Bring the seams together and pin, to hold the stuffing at this position. Turn in the upper edges 1cm (⅜in) and tack. Pleat the upper edge of each arm as shown in Diagram 1, then oversew the edges together as pleated.

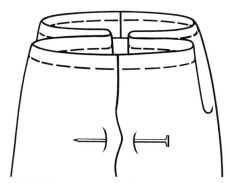

DIAGRAM 1 Showing how to pleat upper edge of arm

Sew these upper edges to the doll at position of the horizontal tacking threads on shoulders having the thumbs pointing inwards. Now sew the edges of the arms which rest against the doll in place at positions of the vertical tacking threads.

Legs

Cut two pairs of leg pieces. Cut two pairs of shoe pieces from felt. Lay out the leg pieces in pairs then tack upper edges of the shoe pieces to lower edges of leg pieces with right sides together and raw edges level. Stitch as tacked then trim seams. Now join centre front and centre back edges of each leg and shoe piece. Trim seams.

Cut two shoe soles from felt and mark on the centre front and back positions. Tack a shoe sole to the lower edge of each shoe, matching the centre front and back points. Stitch as tacked, then trim seams. Turn the legs right side out. Cut two soles from card and trim off the seam allowance all round edges. Place a sole inside each shoe. Stuff the legs to within 4cm (1½in) of upper edges.

Turn in the upper edges 1cm (⅜in) and tack. For the doll's right leg, bring the edges together with a 1cm (⅜in) space between centre front and back seams as shown in Diagram 2. Pin across legs to hold stuffing down as for arms, then oversew upper edges of each leg together. Repeat with left leg, reversing the position of seams.

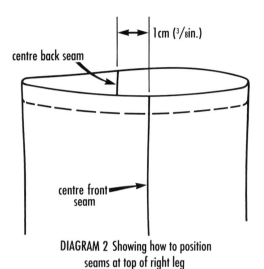

DIAGRAM 2 Showing how to position
seams at top of right leg

For each shoe strap cut a 2x18cm (¾x7in) strip of felt. Fold each in half along length and press, then round off the corners at short ends. Stitch all round near to the edges, allowing long *raw edges* of felt to stretch as you stitch, thus curving the strap to fit round doll's ankles. Sew centres of these curved edges to centre back of legs level with top edges of shoes. Overlap and sew the ends of straps at front then sew on the buttons. Sew trimming round the top edges of the shoes and ribbon bows to fronts.

Now sew upper edges of legs securely to position of the tacking thread on doll's body at front.

THE DOLL'S CLOTHES

Notes: 1cm (⅜in) seams allowed on all clothes pieces unless otherwise stated.

Pantaloons
You will need: 35cm (14in) of 91cm (36in) wide plain cotton fabric; a 65cm (26in) length of lace edging and of narrow ribbon; short lengths of narrow elastic for the legs and broader elastic for the waist; a 65cm (26in) length of ribbon or tape for the elastic casings on the legs.

Cut two pieces as directed on the pattern. Mark on the dotted line at the top edge of each piece. Open up the pieces and trim the upper edges by the dotted lines, forming a curved edge which is higher at the back than the front. Lay pieces out flat so that centre *front* edges face each other, to ensure that you make a pair when sewing on the lace etc.

Narrowly hem the lower edges then sew on lace so that the fancy edge of lace hangs just below hems. Sew ribbon along the top edge of the lace. On the wrong side of each piece, stitch the ribbon or tape in the position shown on pattern. Thread elastic through to fit the doll's legs and secure it at each end of the casings.

Now join pants pieces to each other at centre front and centre back edges. Stitch again at the curves to reinforce, then trim seams at curves. Bring centre seams together and join the inside leg edges of each leg. Clip the seams at curves. Hem the upper edge, taking a 5mm (¼in) then a 1.5cm (⅝in) turning. Thread elastic through to fit the doll's waist.

Petticoat
You will need: 80cm (⅞yd) of 91cm (36in) wide plain cotton fabric; 2.50m (2¾yd) of narrow ribbon; 2m (2¼yd) of lace edging; three snap fasteners or small buttons.

Trim the bodice pattern along the neck edge as shown, then cut out front and back pieces as directed on the pattern. Turn in seam allowance at the shoulder edges and press, then trim 5mm (¼in) off each one. Join front to backs at side edges and trim seams. Now cut and make another bodice in the same way, for the lining. Join lining to bodice at back edges, neck edges then the armhole edges. Trim seams and corners and clip at curves. Turn right side out and press. Now oversew the bodice front to backs at shoulder edges. Join shoulder edges of lining in the same way. Stitch lace round the neck edge folding it at the corners to mitre. Sew ribbon round the top edge of the lace, making a small loop at each corner.

For the skirt front cut a 36x72cm (14¼x28½in) strip of fabric. For the backs cut two 36cm (14¼in) squares. Join each short edge of front to one edge of each back piece. Join the back pieces for centre-back seam taking a 2cm (¾in) seam and leaving a 14cm (5½in) gap at the top for back opening. Press the seam to one side and neaten raw edges of the opening. Narrowly hem skirt's lower edge.

Use your iron to press two fold lines around the skirt, the first one 6cm (2¼in) above the hem and the second 10cm (4in) above the hem. Stitch, 5mm (¼in) away from each fold, forming a tuck. Press the tucks down towards hem. Sew lace and ribbon to lower edge of skirt, letting fancy edge of lace hang just below the hem.

Now gather the upper raw edge of skirt to fit lower edge of the bodice. Sew gathered edge to bodice leaving bodice lining free. Turn in the lower edge of lining and slip-stitch it over the seam line. Sew snaps to back edges of bodice or make buttonholes and sew on buttons. Make a ribbon bow with long ends and sew to waist edge at front.

Dress

You will need: 1.20m (1⅜yd) of 91cm (36in) wide printed cotton fabric, which should be thin enough to gather up tightly; 2.20m (2½yd) of 7cm (2¾in) wide fancy edging and the same amount of 1cm (⅜in) wide feather-edged ribbon and also 5mm (¼in) wide ribbon in a contrast colour; short lengths of narrow elastic for the sleeves; a small buckle and 50cm (20in) of ribbon to fit the width of buckle; three snap fasteners or small buttons.

Cut out front and back bodice pieces as directed on the pattern. Join front to backs at side and shoulder edges and trim seams. Make another bodice in same way for the lining. Join lining to bodice at centre back and neck edges. Trim seams and clip all corners. Turn right side out and press. Tack armholes of lining and bodice together.

Cut two sleeves as directed on pattern. Turn in lower edges 5mm (¼in), then at the fold line indicated on pattern. Press. Stitch lower edge in place, then stitch again 1cm (⅜in) away from this stitching line, forming casing for the elastic. Thread elastic through to fit doll's arm and secure it at each end of the casings. Join underarm edges of each sleeve and neaten raw edges of these seams below the elastic casings. Gather along the top edge of each sleeve as shown on the pattern. Tack sleeves into armholes of dress pulling up the gathers to fit. Stitch as tacked, then stitch again just within first stitching line. Trim seams and neaten.

For the collar, pin, tack and sew fancy edging round the neck edge of bodice, folding it at the corners to mitre as illustrated. Now stitch the ribbons to neck edge in same way as for the petticoat, having the narrow ribbon at centre of the wider ribbon. Sew a ribbon bow to centre front.

For the skirt cut two 36x91cm (14¼x36in)

strips of fabric. Cut one piece in half, to form two 36x45.5cm (14¼x18in) strips for the backs. Join a short edge of each of these back strips to short edges of the long strip. Narrowly hem lower edge and sew on fancy edging above hem so that shaped edge hangs just below the hem. Sew ribbons in place at top edge of the fancy edging to match the neck edge.

Now join the remaining short edges of the skirt, gather waist edge and sew to bodice etc, in same way as for petticoat. Slip the buckle onto the ribbon and pin round waist of bodice having the buckle at centre front. Sew long edges of ribbon in place. Sew snaps to back edges of bodice or sew on buttons and make buttonholes.

Hat

You will need: 20cm (8in) of 91cm (36in) wide plain cotton fabric; 30cm (12in) of 91cm (36in) wide net fabric (such as soft curtain net); 2.40m (2⅝yd) of 1.5cm (⅝in) wide lace trimming; 45cm (18in) length of bias binding to match the hat fabric; 85cm (33½in) length of Rigilene polyester boning; oddments of ribbon etc as available, for trimming the hat.

To make the hat brim Cut a 9x80cm (3½x31½in) strip of plain fabric. Turn in the short edges 1cm (⅜in) and stitch down. Trim off one long edge of the Rigilene strip, then you will be able to pull out the individual plastic rods which will be used for stiffening the hat.

Take three of these plastic rods and hold them together at the ends with bits of sticky tape. Turn in one long edge of the hat brim strip 1cm (⅜in) and press, then stitch down, enclosing the plastic rods as you stitch and letting the rods extend beyond the fabric at each end.

Now cut a 16.5x80cm (6½x31½in) strip of net fabric. Turn in the short edges 1cm (⅜in) and stitch down. Fold the net strip in half along the length, right side outside and enclosing the hat brim strip, with the Rigilene against the fold in the net. Tack all long raw edges together. Stitch, 1cm (⅜in) away from the folded edge.

Now run machined gathering threads along the hat brim strip, 5mm (¼in), 2.5cm (1in) and 5cm (2in) away from the long raw edges. Sew on three rows of lace trimming equally spaced *between* these gathering threads. Pull up the first gathering thread so that this inner

edge of the brim measures 42cm (16½in), then fasten off thread ends securely. Now pull up the other two gathering threads just enough to make the brim lie flat. Fasten off the threads. Bring the short edges of the brim together, remove the sticky tape from plastic rods then tuck in ends of rods lapping them over each other. Slip-stitch the short edges of the brim together.

To make the hat crown Cut an 11x56cm (4¼x22in) strip of the net and also of plain fabric. Turn in the short ends of each and stitch down as for brim. Place the pieces wrong sides together and tack the long edges together. Stitch along the strip 4cm (1½in) away from one long edge (this will be lower edge of hat crown). Stitch again 5mm (¼in) away from this stitching line, forming casing for plastic rods.

Cut two 48cm (19in) long plastic rods and secure them at one end by fixing on a piece of sticky tape. Push the other ends through the casing. Leave both ends of rods protruding 2cm (¾in), securing with sticky tape so that they don't slip back through casing. Bring short edges of fabric strip together and slip-stitch, removing sticky tape from rods and tucking them into casing in same way as for hat brim.

Run gathering threads along upper and lower edges of hat crown. Pull up the upper edge gathers tightly leaving a 5cm (2in) diameter hole, then fasten off. To cover this hole cut a 12cm (4¾in) diameter circle of fabric and of net. Gather them together round the edges. Take a plastic rod and wind it twice round to form a 6cm (2⅜in) diameter circle, trim off excess length and secure ends of rod with sticky tape. Place at centre of fabric circle having net on outside, then pull up gathers tightly and fasten off. Place this circle, gathered side down, on right side of hole at top of hat. Slip-stitch it in place. To neaten raw edges of hole on inside of hat, cut a 6cm (2⅜in) diameter circle of fabric, turn in edge 5mm (¼in) and tack. Sew in place.

To assemble Hat Crown and Brim Pull up gathering thread at lower edge of crown to fit inner edge of brim then tack in place. Stitch as tacked taking a 5mm (¼in) seam. Neaten the raw edges of this seam with the bias binding. Trim hat as desired with a strip of ribbon for a hat band, ribbon rosettes and loops, and fabric flowers if available.

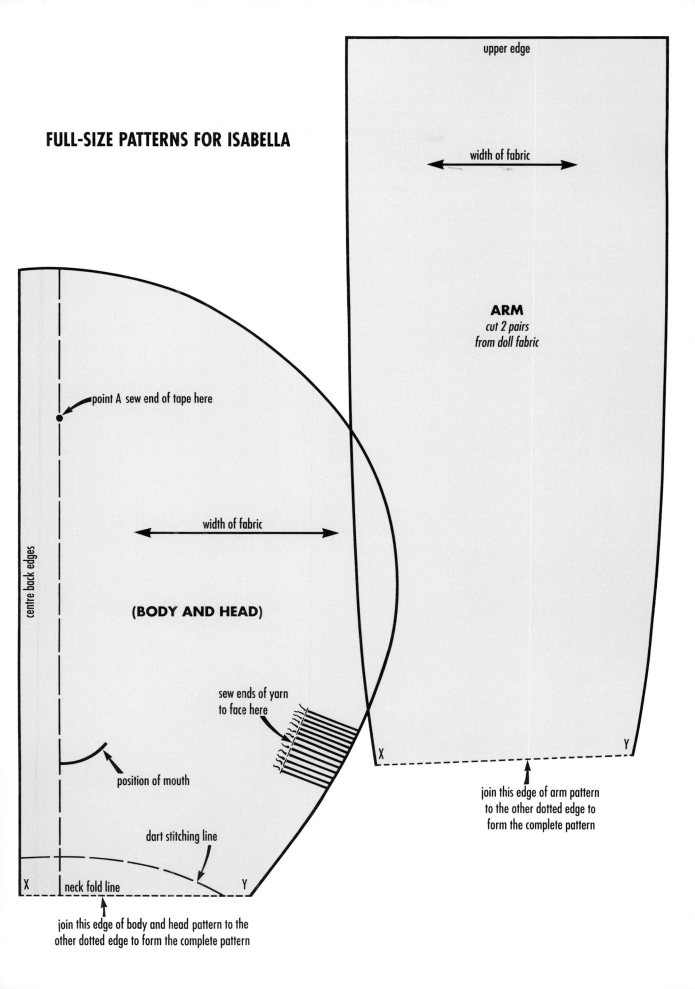

FULL-SIZE PATTERNS FOR ISABELLA

upper edge

width of fabric

ARM
*cut 2 pairs
from doll fabric*

point A sew end of tape here

centre back edges

width of fabric

(BODY AND HEAD)

sew ends of yarn
to face here

position of mouth

X   Y

dart stitching line

X   neck fold line

join this edge of body and head pattern to the
other dotted edge to form the complete pattern

join this edge of arm pattern
to the other dotted edge to
form the complete pattern

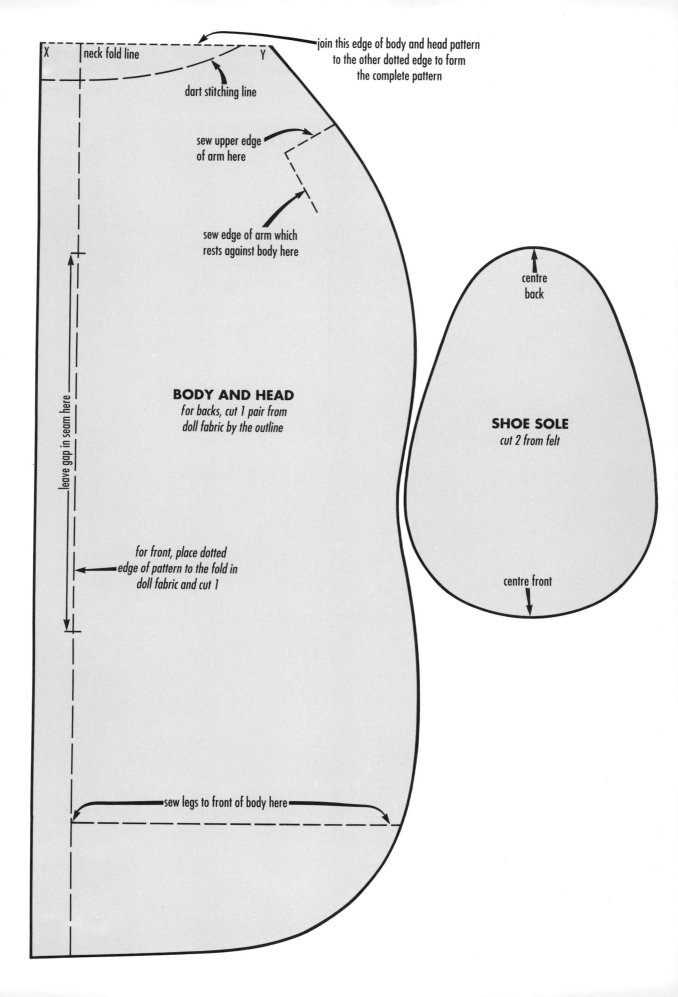

X neck fold line Y

join this edge of body and head pattern
to the other dotted edge to form
the complete pattern

dart stitching line

sew upper edge
of arm here

sew edge of arm which
rests against body here

leave gap in seam here

BODY AND HEAD
*for backs, cut 1 pair from
doll fabric by the outline*

*for front, place dotted
edge of pattern to the fold in
doll fabric and cut 1*

sew legs to front of body here

centre
back

SHOE SOLE
cut 2 from felt

centre front

X

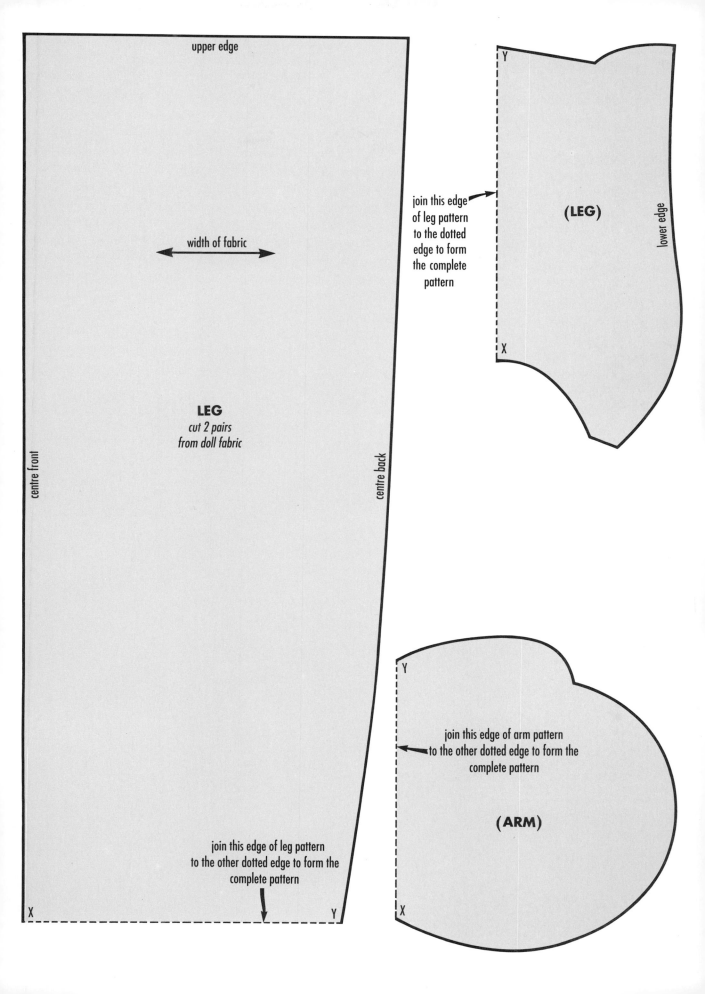

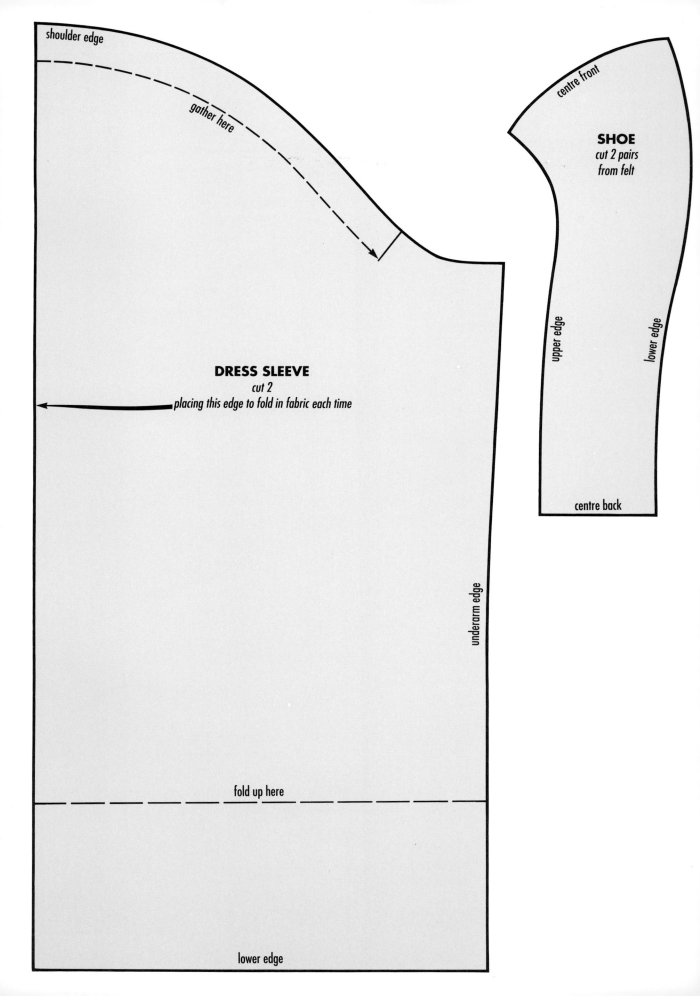

shoulder edge

gather here

centre front

SHOE
*cut 2 pairs
from felt*

upper edge

lower edge

DRESS SLEEVE
cut 2
placing this edge to fold in fabric each time

underarm edge

centre back

fold up here

lower edge

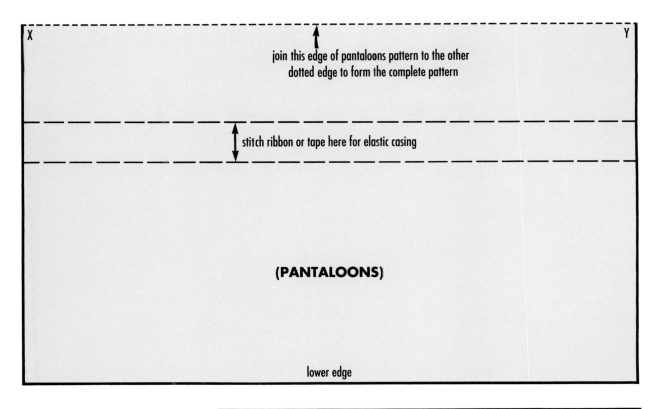

X   Y

join this edge of pantaloons pattern to the other
dotted edge to form the complete pattern

stitch ribbon or tape here for elastic casing

(PANTALOONS)

lower edge

DOLL'S EYE

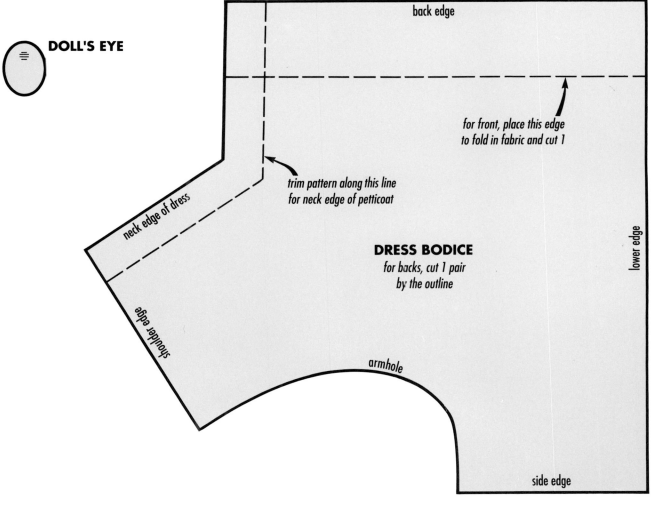

back edge

for front, place this edge
to fold in fabric and cut 1

trim pattern along this line
for neck edge of petticoat

neck edge of dress

shoulder edge

lower edge

DRESS BODICE
for backs, cut 1 pair
by the outline

armhole

side edge

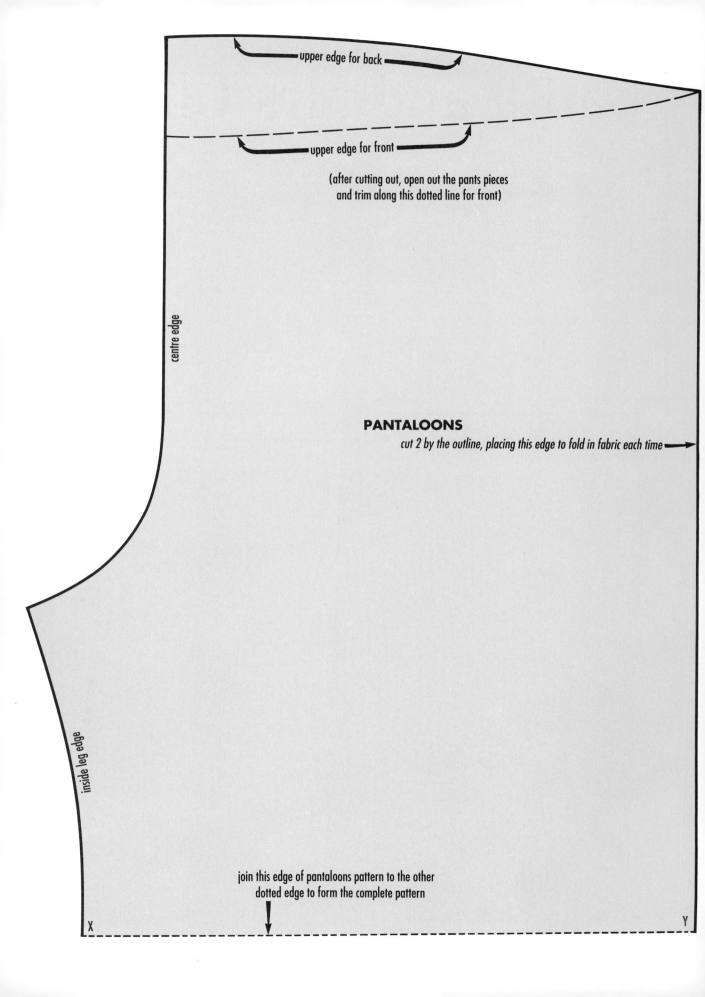

upper edge for back

upper edge for front

(after cutting out, open out the pants pieces
and trim along this dotted line for front)

centre edge

PANTALOONS

cut 2 by the outline, placing this edge to fold in fabric each time

inside leg edge

join this edge of pantaloons pattern to the other
dotted edge to form the complete pattern

X

Y

Santa and Mrs Claus

These cuddly dolls are about 33cm (13in) high. The bodies and limbs are made from circles of fabric, gathered and stuffed, then strung onto elastic.

For both dolls you will need: 50cm (⅝yd) of 91cm (36in) wide printed fabric plus oddments of red, white and black dress-weight cotton fabrics (all fabrics must be thin and soft enough to gather up tightly); 1.60m (1¾yd) of cord elastic about 2mm (1⁄16in) in diameter; pink or white cotton stockinette for heads and hands; small pieces of black felt and white fur fabric; short lengths of narrow elastic and ribbon; oddment of white knitting yarn (any ply) for hair; small amount of stuffing; thin card for circle templates (cuttings off household washing-powder packets

ONE NIGHT BEFORE CHRISTMAS

It was the 24th of December and Santa Claus was preparing for the busiest night of the year. He had already loaded up the sleigh and fed and harnessed the reindeer and now Mrs Claus was fussing about making sure that he had not forgotten anything.

'Now my dear,' she said, 'Have you got your best woolly socks on and the thermal vest I knitted for you?'

'Yes my love,' said Santa with a sigh, knowing exactly what she was going to say next.

'Well my dear,' said Mrs Claus, 'Here is a flask of cocoa and a big bag of my special homemade sticky buns for your midnight snack. I know you get hungry about that time and it's no use climbing down chimneys on an empty stomach.'

Now Santa Claus loved Mrs Claus very much, but unfortunately she made the worst sticky buns in the whole world! Santa had tried feeding the buns to the reindeer but they got quite annoyed because they were into healthy foods and jogging and looking after their teeth. However, Santa Claus took the cocoa and the bag of buns, kissed Mrs Claus goodbye and flew off into the night sky with the reindeer and sleigh.

As they were flying over a field, Santa noticed that the pile of parcels seemed to be getting smaller. 'Can't understand it,' he said, negotiating a quick emergency landing. 'Haven't made any deliveries yet!' On looking around, he saw that there were parcels scattered all over the field. 'Dear, dear, reindeer,' he said, 'Whatever can have happened?' And Santa sent off the deer to round up the parcels while he took a good look at the sleigh.

He soon discovered the problem. Right at the very bottom of the sleigh there was a huge, enormous crack. 'Unhappy Christmas!' cried Santa. 'I'm too far away from base to go back. What's to be done?'

Santa was so upset that he poured a cup of cocoa and absent-mindedly pulled out one of Mrs Claus's sticky buns. He was just about to take a big bite when an idea struck him. 'Sticky solution!' he thought. 'I'll fill the crack with buns!' So he pushed them in place one by one and soon they had all glued themselves firmly together and sealed the crack. Then with the sleigh loaded up again, off they flew into the night with plenty of time to deliver the parcels for Christmas Day.

Santa Claus and the reindeer were quite exhausted when they arrived home, but Mrs Claus had a nice breakfast of bacon and eggs waiting and lots of bran and other boring stuff for the deer. Later on, when they were all sitting comfortably round the fire, Mrs Claus enquired, 'Were the sticky buns to your liking as usual, my dear?'

Santa smiled and winked at the reindeer. 'Couldn't have done without them, my love,' he said, 'They certainly filled a gap!'

But just imagine if Mrs Claus had been a really good sticky bun maker, then nobody would have got any presents that Christmas!

etc); red pencil; a bodkin with a large eye; adhesive.

Notes: 5mm (¼in) seams are allowed unless otherwise stated. Trace the hand and shoe patterns off page onto thin paper, then cut out. Trace the beard pattern onto folded thin paper placing fold to dotted line shown on pattern, then cut out and open up to give full-size pattern.

SANTA CLAUS

The gathered circles

Cut card templates in the following diameters: 13cm (5in), 14cm (5½in), 17cm (6¾in) and 19cm (7½in). Now referring to the table, cut out the number of circles stated in each colour and diameter by drawing round the templates onto the fabric. Several circles may be cut at one time by pinning a few layers of fabric together.

To find centre of each circle, fold it into quarters and mark the centre point with pencil on right side of fabric. Now turn in raw edge of each circle 3mm (⅛in) and gather, taking 1cm (⅜in) long running stitches. Pull up gathers slightly, stuffing the circle lightly and evenly, then pull up gathers as tightly as possible and fasten off securely.

To make the doll

For the head, cut a piece of stockinette 14x15cm (5½x6in) with the most stretch in stockinette going across the 14cm (5½in) measurement. Join the 15cm (6in) edges of the fabric. Gather round one remaining raw edge, pull up gathers tightly and fasten off. Turn head right side out.

For the body, cut a 50cm (20in) length of elastic, fold it in half and make a large knot in the folded end. Stuff head so that it measures about 26cm (10¼in) around, then run a strong gathering thread round 1cm (⅜in) away from remaining raw edge. Pull up the gathers tightly, turning in the raw edge and also enclosing knotted end of body elastic. Fasten off, oversewing securely through the elastic and the gathers in stockinette.

Now using the bodkin and referring to the table, thread the collar and one body circle onto the double body elastic pushing bodkin through the gathers then through the centre marked point of each circle.

For the arms, cut a 30cm (11½in) length of elastic and pass this between the two body elastics. Thread the last two body circles onto the double body elastic. Now divide the body

elastics and thread the leg circles onto each one. Finally thread the arm circles onto each end of the arm elastic. Push all the circles firmly together along each elastic, make large knots in elastics to hold, then trim off excess length. Push a pin through each knot to prevent the circles from slipping off.

Hands

For each hand, cut two pieces from stockinette with most stretch in direction shown on the pattern. Join the pieces leaving wrist edges open. Trim seam, turn right side out and stuff. Gather round the wrist edges. Push the circles away from one knot in the arm elastic and insert a pin through elastic to hold circles away from knot while sewing on the hand. Pull up the wrist gathers in hand tightly, turning in raw edge and enclosing the knotted end of elastic. Fasten off, oversewing securely through elastic and the gathers in stockinette.

Shoes

Pin the shoe pattern to two layers of black felt. Stitch all round, close to edge of the pattern. Before removing the pattern, mark the slit onto the felt. Remove pattern and cut the slit in *one* layer of felt only. Cut out the shoe close to stitching line. Turn right side out through the slit, then stuff firmly. Push the

leg circles away from knots and pin etc, as when attaching hands. Push knotted end of leg elastic inside shoe at the position shown on pattern. Ladder-stitch edges of the slit together and oversew through elastic and felt to hold in place. Check that all the pins have been removed from the elastics.

Face
Use pins, then a pencil to mark eye positions, half way down face and 2.5cm (1in) apart. Using double white sewing thread and a darning needle, take thread through from back of head to marked point of one eye, then take it back through again. Pull tightly to make the eye depression then fasten off. Repeat with other eye. Cut two eyes from black felt. Glue them to the eye depressions. Work a V-shape for mouth in double red thread 1.5cm (⅝in) below the eyes. Colour cheeks with red pencil.

Beard and nose
Cut beard from fur fabric having smooth stroke of fur pile in direction shown. Snip mouth area away carefully. Pin the beard to Santa's face, then sew in place at face edge, upper edge and round the mouth area.

For the nose, cut a 2.5cm (1in) diameter circle of stockinette. Gather and stuff the circle then sew it in place. Colour the nose with red pencil.

Hat
Cut an 18x29cm (7x11½in) strip of red fabric and a 4x29cm (1½x11½in) strip of fur fabric. Join one long edge of the fur strip to one long edge of the fabric strip, right sides together and raw edges level.

Now join short edges of hat. Turn in remaining raw edge of fur fabric and catch it down. Turn hat right side out. Gather up remaining raw edge of red fabric tightly and fasten off.

For the hat bobble, cut, gather and stuff a 4cm (1½in) diameter circle of fur fabric. Push gathered edge of hat inside the bobble, then pull up gathers tightly and fasten off, sewing bobble to hat. Stuff hat very lightly, put on Santa's head as illustrated and catch lower edge to head. Pull top of hat over to one side and catch in place.

MRS CLAUS

Skirt
Cut a 20x91cm (8x36in) strip of printed fabric and join short ends. Hem one long edge. Taking large running stitches, gather up remaining raw edge tightly and fasten off.

The gathered circles
Make these as for Santa, referring to Mrs Claus's table for numbers and colours.

To make the doll
Make exactly as for Santa but thread the skirt onto the body elastics at the position shown in the table.

Hands, shoes and face
Make as for Santa omitting the nose and colouring the nose position with red pencil instead.

Hair
Cut twenty-four 50cm (20in) lengths of white yarn and sew centres of the strands to forehead. Take the strands to each side of head and sew in place level with mouth. Bring all strands together at centre back above neck. Sew them to head. Plait the strands together and tie a ribbon bow round end of plait.

Hat
Cut a 17x70cm (6¾x27½in) strip of printed fabric. Turn in one long edge 4cm (1½in) and stitch it down 5mm (¼in) away from raw edge. Stitch again 5mm (¼in) away from first line of stitching thus forming a casing for the elastic. Thread elastic through to fit the head and secure it at each end of casing.

Join short edges of hat strip. Turn right side out. Gather remaining raw edge and pull up until gathers meet, then fasten off. To cover this raw edge: cut, gather and stuff a 5cm (2in) diameter circle of red fabric and sew to top of hat. Stuff hat lightly and put on Mrs Claus's head with elastic fitting just behind hair. Sew to head near the elastic casing. Sew a ribbon bow to front.

FULL-SIZE PATTERNS FOR SANTA AND MRS CLAUS

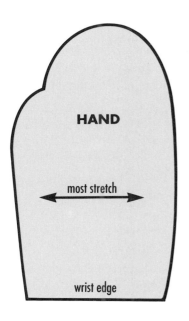

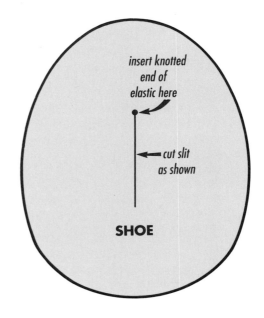

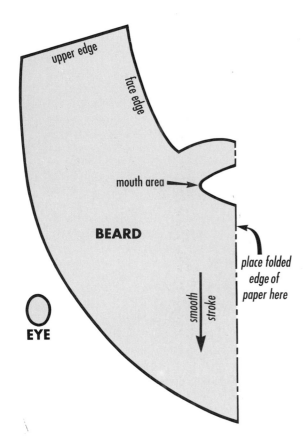

CIRCLES FOR SANTA
IN ORDER OF THREADING

	Number of circles	Colour	Diameter
Collar	1	white	17 cm (6³/₄ in.)
Body	3	red	19 cm (7¹/₂ in.)
Each leg	5	red	14 cm (5¹/₂ in.)
	2	black	14 cm (5¹/₂ in.)
Each arm	4	red	13 cm (5 in.)
	1	white	13 cm (5 in.)

CIRCLES FOR MRS CLAUS
IN ORDER OF THREADING

	Number of circles	Colour	Diameter
Collar	1	print	17 cm (6³/₄ in.)
Body	2	red	19 cm (7¹/₂ in.)
Thread on skirt at this position.			
Body	1	white	19 cm (7¹/₂ in.)
Each leg	7	white	14 cm (5¹/₂ in.)
Each arm	4	red	13 cm (5 in.)
	1	print	13 cm (5 in.)

Best-dressed bear

The smartest Teddy Bear around has two sets of clothes – a duffle coat and scarf for winter and a striped blazer plus flannels and straw boater for those lazy summer days. He measures 46cm (18in) from ears to toes.

For the teddy you will need: 40cm (½yd) of 138cm (54in) wide fawn fur fabric; 350g (¾lb) of stuffing; small pieces of light brown felt for foot and paw pads, dark brown for the eyes and nose; black double-knitting yarn for mouth; dressmaker's graph paper ruled into 5cm (2in) squares; strong fawn thread.

Notes: Draw patterns onto the graph paper from scaled down diagram noting that each square on diagram = 5cm (2in). Cut out all fur fabric pieces with smooth stroke of fur pile going in direction shown by arrows on each pattern piece. 5mm (¼in) seams are allowed on all pieces unless otherwise stated.

BASIC TEDDY

The Head

Cut a pair of head pieces and one head gusset from fur fabric. Bring the edges of the darts together in each head piece and stitch darts

TEDDIES

There once was a teddy named Fraser,
Who wore a straw hat and a blazer;
He bought a new boat,
The boat didn't float,
That water-logged teddy named Fraser.

There once was a teddy named Joe,
Who stood for a week in the snow;
The silly young feller,
Forgot his umbrella,
That snow-covered teddy named Joe.

as shown. Join head pieces from point A down to the neck edge. Now join head gusset to head pieces matching points A, over top of head to neck edge. Turn head right side out and stuff firmly. Using strong thread, gather round neck edge, pull up gathers tightly and fasten off. Lay the head aside.

Arms

Cut two pairs of arm pieces from fur fabric and join them in pairs leaving the inner edges open. Turn right side out and stuff, then tack the inner edges together. Lay the arms aside.

Legs

Cut two pairs of leg pieces from fur fabric and two soles from light brown felt. Join the centre front and centre back edges of each leg. Clip the seams at positions indicated. Join edges of the soles to lower edges of legs by back-stitching the seams all round, matching points B and C. Turn legs right side out and stuff, then bring front and back seams together and tack across the upper edges. Lay the legs aside.

Body

Cut one pair of body fronts from fur fabric. Join centre front seam. Sew the inner edges of the arms to side edges as shown on the pattern having all raw edges level and curves of the arms pointing up towards the neck edge.

Cut one pair of body back pieces from fur fabric. Join the centre back edges. Cut one body base piece from fur fabric. Sew the curved edge of the base piece to lower edge of the body piece, matching points D and E. Now back-stitch upper edges of legs to front edge of the base piece with raw edges level and toes pointing away from the body piece. Now let the legs flop downwards away from the body.

Tack the body front to back at the side edges then stitch the seams. Turn body right side out, then turn in lower edge of the body front and slip-stitch it over the seam line, thus enclosing top raw edges of legs. Stuff body firmly then gather up the neck edge in same way as for the head.

Place the head in position on top of the body matching the gathered portions.

Ladder-stitch the head to body using strong thread, working round two or three times for strength.

Ears, Face and Paw Pads

Cut four ear pieces from fur fabric. Join them in pairs leaving the lower edges open. Turn right side out and oversew lower edges together pulling stitches tightly to gather slightly. Sew to head on either side, lapping the gusset about 1cm (⅜in) and having the ears in line with the arms.

Cut two paw pads from felt to match soles of the feet and sew them in place at ends of the arms as illustrated. Cut four eyes from dark brown felt and oversew them together in pairs round the edges. Work a highlight in white thread on each eye as shown in the illustration. Pin the eyes in position on either side of the head gusset just above the level of the snout.

Trim fur pile shorter below the snout and around mouth area. Using black yarn, make a V-shape, worked in two long stitches, about 2.5cm (1in) below snout, starting and finishing off the yarn underneath position of each eye. Now sew the eyes in position, using a little adhesive if desired at centre of each, to hold in place while sewing. Cut two nose pieces from dark brown felt and oversew them together as for the eyes. Sew the nose to end of snout.

THE CLOTHES

Note: 1cm (⅜in) seams are allowed on all garments unless otherwise stated.

Winter Coat
You will need: 40cm (½yd) of 91cm (36in) wide felt; five buttons about 13mm (½in) in diameter and a snap fastener.

Cut two pockets from felt. Stitch round the edges of pocket flaps as shown on pattern. Fold the flaps down at fold lines and press. Cut one pair of coat front pieces and stitch pockets to fronts leaving the flaps free, as shown on the pattern. Cut the coat back from felt. Join fronts to back at shoulder and side edges and press the seams open.

Turn up hem edge 1cm (⅜in) and tack, then stitch in place. Turn in centre front edges 2cm (¾in) and tack, then stitch in place. Stitch through folded edges of centre fronts also. Cut two collar pieces, placing the edge of pattern indicated to fold in felt each time. Join the pieces round the edges taking a 5mm (¼in) seam and leaving the neck edges open. Trim corners, then turn collar right side out and press. Stitch neck edge of one collar piece to right side of neck edge of coat having raw edges level and taking a 5mm (¼in) seam. Turn in remaining neck edge of collar and slip-stitch it over the seam. Machine-stitch round the outer edge of collar.

Cut two sleeves placing pattern to fold in felt each time as indicated. Join the underarm edges of each sleeve and press open. Turn in wrist edges 1cm (⅜in) and tack, then stitch in place.

Now tack the armhole edges of sleeves to armholes of coat, right sides together, raw edges level, matching the underarm and the side seams and easing sleeves to fit. Stitch seams, then stitch again just within first line of stitching. Trim seams close to this line of stitching.

Machine-stitch round the buttonholes on left front as shown on the pattern, then cut buttonholes open. Sew buttons to right front of coat to correspond with buttonholes. Sew a button to each pocket through the flap. Sew the snap fastener to ends of collar to fasten.

Winter Scarf
You will need: Oddments of double-knitting yarn and a pair of No 10 (3¼mm, USA 3) knitting needles.

Abbreviations: st-st = stocking stitch; st(s) = stitch(es); K = knit; P = purl. LG = light green; G = green; R = red.

Using LG, cast on 10 sts. 1st row: Increase K wise into every st – 20sts. Beginning with a P row, st-st 3 rows. *Join on R and st-st 2 rows. Join on G and st-st 2 rows. Continue with R and st-st 2 rows. Continue with LG and st-st 4 rows. Repeat from * 18 times, carrying the yarns loosely up side of work when changing colours.

Now work the R, G, R, sequence of stripes once more. Using LG, st-st 3 rows. Next row: (P 2 tog) repeat to end – 10sts. Break off yarn leaving a long end, thread it through remaining sts, pull up tightly and fasten off.

To make up
Join long edges of scarf leaving cast on edge open. Turn right side out, pushing gathered-up end through with knob of a knitting needle. Gather round the cast on edge, pull up tightly and fasten off. Make two tassels using LG and sew them to ends of scarf.

Summer Pants
You will need: 30cm (⅜yd) of 91cm (36in) wide fabric; a 38cm (15in) length of elastic.

Cut one pair of pants pieces and mark the dotted 'side' line on each one with a tacking thread. Join the inside leg edges of each pants piece. Turn right side out. Place this seam in line with the tacking thread on each pants piece, then press the front and back creases.

Pin the inside leg seams together, then join the pants pieces to each other at centre front and centre back edges. Clip and trim seams at curves. Hem the waist edge taking a 5mm (¼in), then a 1cm (⅜in) turning. Thread the elastic through. Narrowly hem the ankle edges.

Blazer
You will need: 60cm (⅝yd) of 91cm (36in) wide striped dress-weight fabric; 30cm (⅜yd) of 91cm (36in) wide lightweight iron-on interfacing; three small buttons.

First, iron the interfacing onto the wrong side of half of the dress fabric. This piece will be for the right side of the blazer, the remainder will be used for the lining pieces and will be referred to as the 'lining' fabric. The stripes should run vertically on the front and back blazer pieces.
From the blazer fabric cut one pair of blazer front pieces and mark positions of

pockets on the wrong side of each piece. From blazer fabric cut four upper and four lower pocket pieces matching run of the stripes on pockets to stripes on front blazer pieces. Join the pocket pieces in pairs taking 5mm (¼in) seams and leaving gaps for turning. Trim seams and corners, then turn right side out and slip-stitch gaps. Slip-stitch the pockets to blazer fronts at the marked positions.

Cut one blazer back piece from blazer fabric placing the edge indicated to fold in fabric, then join fronts to back at side edges. From the lining fabric cut one pair of fronts and one back and join them at side edges as for the blazer. Now join lining to blazer at back neck edges; then front neck edges, lapels, centre front and lower edges. Trim seams and clip at the curves, then turn right side out and press. Join front shoulder edges of blazer and also of lining to back shoulder edges. Tack the armhole edges of lining and blazer together.

Cut two sleeves from blazer fabric placing

edge indicated to fold in fabric each time and having stripes in the direction shown on the pattern. Join the underarm edges of each sleeve. Now sew armhole edges of sleeves to the armhole edges of blazer taking 5mm (¼in) seams. Stitch again close to seam lines, then trim seams close to these lines of stitching. Oversew raw edges of the armholes to neaten. Hem the wrist edges of sleeves taking 5mm (¼in), then 1cm (⅜in) turnings.

For the collar, cut a 6x25cm (2⅜x10in) strip of the blazer fabric having stripes running parallel with the short edges. Join long edges and across short edges taking a 5mm (¼in) seam and leaving a gap for turning. Trim seam and corners, turn right side out, then slip-stitch the gap and press collar. Now pin the long seamed edge of collar against back and front neck edges of blazer, edge to edge, easing the collar to fit. Oversew the edges together as pinned, on the right side of blazer, so that oversewing stitches will be underneath the collar when collar is turned down. Fold down lapels at fold lines and press.

Make three buttonholes in left front edge of the blazer as shown on pattern and sew buttons to other edge to correspond. Alternatively, sew the buttons to left front and fasten the blazer with snap fasteners.

Cravat
Use a 20x60cm (8x24in) strip of thin soft fabric and make as for the blazer collar.

Straw Boater
You will need: 30cm (⅜yd) of 91cm (36in) wide pale yellow coarsely woven fabric, to resemble straw; 60cm (⅝yd) of striped or plain ribbon about 1.5cm (⅝in) in width; short length of narrow tape or ribbon; thin strong card (cuttings off washing-powder packets etc); sticky tape; adhesive.

For the hat brim, cut a 21cm (8¼in) diameter circle of card, then cut a 13cm (5in) diameter circle from the centre, forming the inner edge of the brim. Stick the brim onto a piece of fabric then cut out fabric 1cm (⅜in) away from the outer and inner edges of brim. Turn and stick this extra fabric to the other side of the card, clipping the inner edges at intervals. Make another brim in the same way and stick the two together, sandwiching the raw edges of fabric between them. Pinch the card circles together firmly round the edges until the glue dries.

For the side of the hat crown, cut a 4x41cm (1⅝x16in) strip of card. Join the short ends with sticky tape to form a circle. Cover the card with a strip of fabric in the same way as for brim, turning the raw edges of fabric to inside and butting the short ends neatly. Now cut another strip of card slightly shorter than first strip and stick this to the inside of first strip of card to cover the raw edges of the fabric. Stick this completed piece securely to the inner edge of the hat brim. To make sure that the hat side piece is securely held to the brim, stick a strip of ribbon or tape round inside, to hold the edges of both pieces together.

For top of hat crown, cut a 13cm (5in) diameter circle of card and cover with fabric in the same way as for other pieces. Stick it securely to top of the hat, then glue a slightly smaller circle of card to the inside to cover the raw edges of fabric.

Stick ribbon round the hat, joining the ends at one side. Make a small ribbon bow and stick it to the ribbon join.

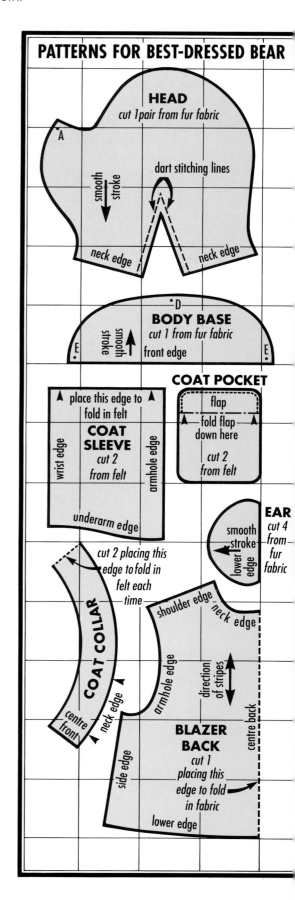

PATTERNS FOR BEST-DRESSED BEAR

HEAD
cut 1 pair from fur fabric

smooth stroke

dart stitching lines

neck edge   neck edge

BODY BASE
cut 1 from fur fabric
front edge

smooth stroke

COAT POCKET

place this edge to fold in felt

COAT SLEEVE
cut 2 from felt

wrist edge   armhole edge

underarm edge

flap
fold flap down here
cut 2 from felt

EAR
cut 4 from fur fabric

smooth stroke
lower edge

cut 2 placing this edge to fold in felt each time

COAT COLLAR

centre front   neck edge

shoulder edge   neck edge

armhole edge

direction of stripes

centre back

BLAZER BACK
cut 1 placing this edge to fold in fabric

side edge

lower edge

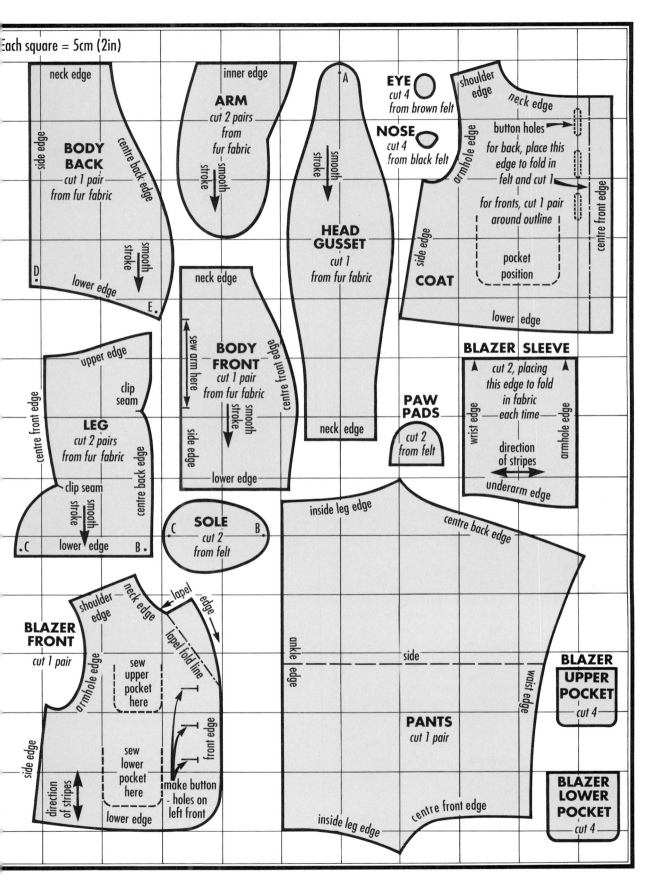

Each square = 5cm (2in)

neck edge

BODY BACK
cut 1 pair
from fur fabric

side edge

centre back edge

smooth stroke

smooth stroke

lower edge

D

E

inner edge

ARM
cut 2 pairs
from fur fabric

smooth stroke

smooth stroke

A

HEAD GUSSET
cut 1
from fur fabric

neck edge

EYE
cut 4
from brown felt

NOSE
cut 4
from black felt

shoulder edge

neck edge

armhole edge

side edge

button holes
for back, place this edge to fold in felt and cut 1
for fronts, cut 1 pair around outline

pocket position

centre front edge

COAT

lower edge

BLAZER SLEEVE
cut 2, placing this edge to fold in fabric each time
direction of stripes

wrist edge

armhole edge

underarm edge

upper edge

clip seam

LEG
cut 2 pairs
from fur fabric

centre front edge

centre back edge

clip seam

smooth stroke

lower edge

C

B

neck edge

BODY FRONT
cut 1 pair
from fur fabric

sew arm here

centre front edge

smooth stroke

side edge

lower edge

neck edge

SOLE
cut 2
from felt

C

B

PAW PADS
cut 2
from felt

BLAZER FRONT
cut 1 pair

shoulder edge

neck edge

lapel

edge

lapel fold line

armhole edge

sew upper pocket here

sew lower pocket here

make button - holes on left front

front edge

side edge

direction of stripes

lower edge

inside leg edge

centre back edge

ankle edge

side

PANTS
cut 1 pair

waist edge

inside leg edge

centre front edge

BLAZER UPPER POCKET
cut 4

BLAZER LOWER POCKET
cut 4

Oceans of Toys

You don't need any special patterns to create this collection of small sea creatures. They're all delightfully simple to sew using circular and rectangular pieces of fabric which are gathered, stitched and stuffed. There are shells of various sizes, the largest two are about 5cm (2in) across, one contains a pearl, the other a cockle. The fish is 11.5cm (4½in) long, the starfish 10cm (4in) across, the crab is 15cm (6in) wide across the claws and the octopus measures about 28cm (11in) across. The mermaid is 35.5cm (14in) in length and to complete the scene you can also make some pebbles and attach a limpet to one of them.

You will need: Oddments of cotton fabrics, printed and plain as shown in the illustration; pink or white cotton stockinette; stuffing; cord elastic about 2mm (¹⁄₁₆in) in diameter; black beads for eyes – small, about 2mm (¹⁄₁₆in) in diameter and large, about 5mm (¼in) in diameter; thin card for the circle templates, cut off household cereal and washing-powder packets etc; small guipure flowers; brown permanent marker pens; strong thread for gathering; transparent snap fasteners; Velcro hook and loop fastener; a scrap of black felt and red pencil for mermaid's face; fancy green yarn for mermaid's hair; small pearl beads for her necklace; adhesive.

Notes: All measurements for the circles are given as the *diameters* of the circles. Use compasses to draw the required sized circle onto the card, cut out the card circle then mark on the diameter for future reference. Use a pencil to draw round the edge of the circle onto the fabric, then cut out the fabric circle.

When measurements are given for rectangular shapes, cut paper patterns to the specified sizes to save having to measure the fabric each time.

When taking large oversewing stitches around some of the shapes (for example when making the shells), pass the point of the needle through a bit of the fabric at the outer edge of the shape, so that the stitch will remain in position and not slip off. (See the Diagram, which shows this quite clearly.)

Take 3mm (⅛in) seams and turnings unless otherwise stated.

To gather and stuff a circle

Using the strong thread, take small running stitches round each of the smaller circles, 3mm (⅛in) away from the raw edge. Pull up the gathers slightly and stuff the circle at the same time to make a nice rounded shape, but do not stuff too firmly. Pull up the gathers tightly to close completely, then fasten off the gathering thread. If working with a very large circle of fabric, you will need to take larger running stitches in order to be able to pull up the gathers as tightly as possible.

To cover the gathered raw edges, another circle of fabric must be sewn to the stuffed shape. When instructions are given to do this, turn in the raw edge of the covering circle 3mm (⅛in) and tack, then sew the circle in place centrally over the gathers.

SHELLS
Pink striped shell with pearl inside

For each half of the shell, cut, gather and stuff a 12cm (4¾in) circle of fabric. Secure a double length of sewing thread at a position at the edge of the stuffed shape. Take the sewing thread around the shape to divide it in half, then fasten off the thread after pulling it tightly, at the position where it was first secured. Work three more oversewing stitches in the same way on each side of the first stitch as shown in the Diagram.

To cover the gathered raw edges of each shell, cut a 4cm (1⅝in) circle and trim it to an oval shape. Turn in and tack the raw edge, then sew the circle in place. Sew a pearl bead to the flat side of one shell half. Place the shell

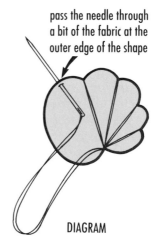

pass the needle through a bit of the fabric at the outer edge of the shape

DIAGRAM

MERMAID'S EYE

MORWENNA
THE LONELY MERMAID

Once upon a time, in a deep dark blue ocean, there lived a little mermaid called Morwenna. Now because Morwenna's home was in a secret cave, she hardly ever met any other creatures and this made her very sad and lonely.

One day a little pink crab came scurrying by. He stopped to be polite. 'Evening,' he said, 'Or is it morning? I'm never quite sure.'

'It's afternoon,' replied Morwenna, surprised indeed to have a visitor.

'My name is Crusty Crab,' said the crab, 'but please tell me why you look so sad, little mermaid?' So Morwenna told Crusty how lonely she was in her secret cave with no friends to play with. 'Then', announced Crusty, dancing into the cave on his toes, 'I shall stay for a while and try to come up with an idea. I'm jolly good at finding ideas you know.'

Morwenna could hardly believe it when she saw a plump green octopus coming towards the cave. He stopped to be polite. 'Ollie Octopus is the name,' he said. 'But why do you both look so worried?' Crusty and Morwenna told Ollie about the problem and he very kindly promised to help. 'I am quite good at thinking,' he said bobbing into the cave on his eight legs. 'After all I do have a thinking cap on my head as you may have noticed.'

The very next minute, before you could even say 'shivery seals' a fat stripy fish came gliding along. He stopped to be polite. 'Freddy Fish at your service,' he said swimming into the cave. 'I just happened to be passing and noticed that you all looked very worried. Have you got a problem?'

'Yes we have,' said the three together, 'And we haven't found the answer yet, though we've tried very hard.'

'Well,' said Freddy, floating in and out of the wavy weeds, 'I have nothing else to do except wander about, so in my spare time I'm sure I can help to sort things out.'

Now a tiny blue starfish just happened to be on her way home and couldn't help overhearing the chattering coming from Morwenna's secret cave. She stopped to be polite. 'Good day, I'm Stella Starfish,' she said scuttling into the cave. 'What is going on here?'

'We are pondering' replied Ollie. 'A most difficult dilemma indeed.'

'In that case,' said Stella, 'I would like to ponder with you, even though I don't exactly know what a dilemma is, I am very good at pondering.'

So there they were, Crusty Crab trying to get an idea, Ollie Octopus thinking hard, Freddie Fish taking lots of time and Stella Starfish pondering. It seemed that between them they would *surely* manage to solve Morwenna's problem.

Just then, there was a sudden movement in the sand and out popped a tiny cockle that nobody had even noticed. The cockle was not at all polite, in fact he was very rude. 'Noise, noise, noise,' he grumbled crossly. 'Really, can't a cockle get any peace and quiet around here? With all this non-stop chattering and to-ing and fro-ing, I can't get any sleep. And who said that you could have a party anyway?'

'But we are not having a party,' explained Morwenna. 'You see, we are all trying to think of a way for me to find some friends so that I won't be lonely.'

'Doddering Dolphins, you are a silly lot' cried the cockle. 'Even a cock-eyed cuttle fish could see that you don't *have* a problem!'

'We don't?' they all exclaimed in surprise. 'Of course not,' tutted the cockle. 'Don't you realise, little mermaid, that you have now found four friends – and very noisy friends they are I might add. Now if you don't mind, I need my beauty sleep.'

With that, the cross little cockle snapped back into his shell, snuggled deep into the sand and fell fast asleep. And while the cockle snoozed, Morwenna's four friends decided to stay in her secret cave, so that she would never, ever be lonely again.

halves together and oversew at back edges to form a hinge. Sew two snap fasteners to the shell halves so the shell can be closed.

Blue striped shell with cockle inside

Make as for Shell with Pearl. For the cockle, cut, gather and stuff a 4cm (1⅝in) circle of stockinette fabric. Sew on two small beads for the eyes on top of the gathered shape. Sew a 2cm (¾in) circle of fabric under the cockle to cover the gathered raw edge.

Loose half shells

Make as for other shell halves using a variety of smaller-sized striped fabric circles.

THE CRAB

Body

Cut and gather a 20cm (8in) circle of pink spotted fabric. Stuff quite lightly to make a flattish shape, then pull up gathers tightly and fasten off. For the eyes sew on two large beads near to the edge of the crab and 2cm (¾in) apart, taking sewing threads through crab to gathers underneath and pulling them tightly to depress the beads into the fabric. Sew a 5cm (2in) circle underneath crab to cover the gathered raw edge.

Front claws (make two)

For each claw, cut two 4.5x9cm (1¾x3½in) strips of fabric. Join them, leaving seam open at one short edge and rounding off the corners at other short edges to a pointed V-shape. Trim corners, turn right side out and stuff. Gather round raw edge and pull up tightly, turning in the raw edge, then fasten off. Divide each claw into two sections by securing sewing thread halfway down claw then winding it tightly round and round at the centre of the length. Fasten off.

Take a long oversewing stitch round the pointed end of each claw to divide it into two pincers in the same way as directed for the shells. Bend each claw at the centre and catch first and second sections together at the bend to hold at an angle. Sew the gathered ends of claws to the crab at each side of the eyes.

Legs (make eight)

For each leg cut two 3x6cm (1¼x2⅜in) strips of fabric. Seam, turn, stuff and gather raw edge as for claws. Divide each leg into three sections by winding round sewing thread in same way as for the claws. Sew the legs to sides of body, four at each side. Sew a few guipure flowers to top of body.

THE FISH

For the body cut a 22cm (8¾in) semi-circle of multicoloured striped fabric. Fold it in half and join the straight raw edges, rounding off the corner at centre point of semi-circle. Trim off this corner, turn right side out and gather round the raw edge. Stuff, pull up the gathers tightly and fasten off. (Note when making the rest of fish that the seam will run underneath body of fish.)

Sew on large beads for the eyes taking the stitches through from one side of fish to the other and pulling thread tightly before fastening off. For the mouth work a large oversewing stitch round pointed end of fish using black thread.

For the tail, cut a 10cm (4in) circle of fabric. Fold it in half and join the raw edges leaving a gap for turning. Turn right side out, stuff lightly then slip-stitch the gap. Gather at centre of the semi-circle then tie thread tightly round the gathers. Sew the tail to gathered end of the fish having curved edge of tail against the fish gathers.

For each fin (make two), cut a 10cm (4in) semi-circle. Fold in half and stitch etc as for the tail. Gather one straight edge of one fin and sew to seam line under fish. In the same way, sew the other fin on top of fish.

THE OCTOPUS

Body

Cut a 26cm (10¼in) circle of green printed fabric, then cut away one quarter of the circle and discard the quarter. Join short straight edges of remaining three-quarter circle, rounding off in a generous curve at the centre point of the circle. Trim seam and turn right side out. Gather round raw edge stuffing the body firmly, then pull up gathers tightly and fasten off. Sew on two large beads for eyes at position illustrated in the same way as for the crab, spacing them 2.5cm (1in) apart. Work a V-shape for the mouth in black thread below the eyes as illustrated.

To cover the gathered raw edge underneath body, cut an 8cm (3in) circle of green printed fabric. Turn in and tack the raw edge but do not sew in place. Cut eight 12cm (4¾in) lengths of elastic and make a knot in one end of each. Now place the knotted ends of elastics equally spaced, round the wrong side of the edge of the fabric circle, having the lengths of elastic going away from the edge of the circle. Oversew the elastics securely to edge of circle. Now slip-stitch the circle in place on the body, then oversew each elastic securely to the body fabric. Cut and gather a 12cm (4¾in) circle of plain green fabric and sew it to the head. Then sew on a guipure flower, to cover the gathered raw edge.

Legs

Cut twenty-four 9cm (3½in) green printed fabric circles and sixteen plain green fabric circles. Fold each one into quarters and snip off corners at centre of circle to make a tiny hole. Turn in the raw edges of circles, gather and stuff lightly then pull up gathers tightly and fasten off.

Now thread three patterned and two plain circles alternately onto each elastic and knot the ends of elastics. Push pins through elastics above the knots to prevent the circles from slipping off.

Feet

Cut eight 12cm (4¾in) semi-circles of plain green fabric. Fold each in half to make a semi-circle, then fold again into quarters and join straight edges, rounding off corner at centre of semi-circle. Trim corner and turn right side out. Turn in the raw edges, gather and stuff, then pull up gathers tightly around knotted ends of leg elastics and fasten off. Oversew through gathers in feet and elastics to hold in place.

PEBBLES AND LIMPET

Use sandy- or stone-coloured fabric with a coarse weave for the pebbles, gathering and stuffing circles of different sizes. Sew circles of same fabric underneath the stones to cover the gathered raw edges. Mark lines on the pebbles with brown pens as shown in the illustration.

For the limpet cut a 10cm (4in) semi-circle of pink fabric and stitch on lines radiating from centre point of circle to outer edge. Stitch a couple of lines also, parallel to curved edge of semi-circle. Fold the semi-circle in half and join the straight raw edges. Turn and stuff then gather up the raw edge tightly and fasten off. Sew on a circle of furry Velcro to cover the raw edge, then sew a circle of hooked Velcro to one pebble to fix the limpet in place.

THE STARFISH

For the body, cut, gather and stuff a 9cm (3½in) circle of blue fabric. Sew on large beads for eyes as for the crab, spacing them 1cm (⅜in) apart. For the legs cut five 8cm (3¼in) circles. Fold each one into quarters, then fold the side edges of each quarter in towards each other, overlapping them 5mm

(¼in). Oversew all the raw edges of each leg together. Sew these raw edges underneath starfish's body so that raw edges of corners just touch each other. Sew on a 4.5cm (1¾in) circle to cover all raw edges.

THE MERMAID
Body and head
Cut a 12cm wide x 22cm long (4¾x8¾in) strip of stockinette with most stretch in stockinette going across the 12cm (4¾in) width. Join the long edges. Gather round one short edge, pull up tightly and fasten off. Turn right side out and stuff, then run a gathering thread round 1cm (⅜in) away from the remaining raw edge but do not pull up.

To shape the neck, tie strong thread very tightly round, 11cm (4¼in) down from gathered top of head. Sew thread ends into neck. Cut an 18cm (7in) circle of white fabric, gather and stuff circle, then insert it inside the lower gathered edge of body. Now pull up the body gathers tightly, turning in the raw edges and also enclosing the knotted end of a 30cm (12in) length of elastic. Oversew through gathers and the elastic to hold in place.

Tail
Cut ten circles of green printed fabric, ranging from 8 to 17cm (3⅛ to 6⅝in) with 1cm (⅜in) intervals between each one. Gather and stuff these circles in same way as for Octopus legs (see page 60). Thread the circles onto the body elastic in sequence from large to small pushing them close together. Knot the end of the elastic then push a pin through elastic above the knot to prevent the circles from slipping off. Sew the largest gathered tail circle to lower end of the body where it touches the body.

Tail fin
Cut a 12cm (4¾in) circle of pink fabric, fold it in half and join round the curved edges leaving a gap at centre of curved seam. Turn right side out and stuff lightly, then slip-stitch the gap, enclosing the knotted end of the tail elastic at centre of gap. Sew through the gathers and the elastic to secure. Gather up through centre of the fin, pull up gathers tightly and fasten off, then oversew around the gathers.

Arms
For each arm cut a 6cm wide x 14cm long (2⅜x5½in) strip of stockinette with most stretch going across the 6cm (2⅜in) width. Join the long edges of each strip and across both short ends rounding off all corners and leaving a gap in seam for turning. Trim corners, turn and stuff, then ladder-stitch gaps. Tie a thread tightly round each arm to shape wrists, 3.5cm (1⅜in) away from one end of each. Sew the thread ends into wrists. Sew the other ends of the arms to body at each side 1cm (⅜in) down from the neck.

Face
Cut the eyes from black felt using the pattern. Glue them in place, half-way down the face and 2cm (¾in) apart. Work a straight pink stitch for the mouth, 1cm (⅜in) below the eyes. Work a tiny vertical stitch below the centre of the mouth stitch, looping it around the first stitch to pull it downwards into a V-shape. Colour the cheeks and nose with red pencil.

Necklace
Thread two strands of pearl beads onto the strong sewing thread and tie them round neck. Catch them to the neck at back and to the shoulders also.

Hair
For the front portion of the hair cut about twenty 50cm (20in) long strands of yarn. Stitch centre of the strands to a 1x6cm (⅜x2½in) strip of stockinette. Turn in the ends of the strip and pin it to centre parting of head starting at forehead. Tie lengths of thread round strands at each side of head to hold them together while doing the back hair. To cover back of the head cut three 3m (3¼yd) lengths of yarn and fold them in half. Plait the strands together loosely. Now starting at centre back of head, sew plait to head coiling it round and round to cover the portion of the head behind first strands. Sew front strands in place as pinned at centre parting, then catch them to sides of head, level with mouth.

Headband
Cut a 4x15cm (1½x6in) strip of pink fabric and join the long edges. Turn right side out. Gather through the fabric at centre of strip and pull up tight, then sew on a pearl bead. Push a bit of stuffing in, on each side of the centre gathers, then gather again 2cm (¾in) away from each side of the first gathers. Sew on beads as before. Continue like this, working towards each end of the strip, then turn in and join ends and sew on the last bead. Sew the headband to the mermaid's head as illustrated.

Humpty Dumpty

Humpty measures 46cm (18in) from top to toe. There are full-size patterns for all the shaped pieces while the cap, arms and legs are made from circular and straight strips of fabric for which measurements are given.

You will need: 40cm (½yd) of 91cm (36in) wide pink cotton fabric; 40cm (½yd) of 91cm (36in) wide striped cotton fabric (with stripes running down length); 700g (1½lb) stuffing; 1.60m (1¾yd) of ric-rac braid; a 24x30cm

(9½x12in) piece of felt for the feet; 1.30m (1½yd) of 5cm (2in) wide ribbon; 40cm (½yd) of 91cm (36in) wide plain fabric; oddments of Polyester wadding and iron-on interfacing for cap; a 20g (¾oz) ball of yellow double-knitting yarn and a pair of 3¾mm (No 9, USA 4) knitting needles for hair; scraps of peach, pink, black and blue felt; adhesive.

Notes: When pattern pieces are marked with direction of *width* of fabric, take care to cut out piece accordingly. 5mm (¼in) seams are allowed on all pieces unless otherwise stated. Trace patterns off the pages and mark on all details.

Knitting abbreviations: K = knit; st = stitch.

Arms

Cut two pairs of hand pieces from pink fabric. Join them in pairs from wrist edge at thumb side of pieces, stitching just a little of the seam.

For each sleeve cut a 9x24cm (3½x9½in) strip of striped fabric with stripes running parallel with the short edges. Gather one long edge of each sleeve to fit wrist edge of each hand. Sew in place with right sides together and raw edges level. Join remainder of hand seams and short edges of sleeves. Trim seams around hands. Turn right side out. Stuff hands firmly, then sleeves lightly. Bring raw edges of each sleeve together with sleeve seam at one side and gather to measure 6cm (2⅜in). Sew ric-rac round wrists.

Head and Body
Front piece

Cut two head pieces from pink fabric and mark mouth lines on right side of fabric, taking care to mark them as a pair.

Cut two body pieces from striped fabric and mark the leg lines on right side of each one. Join the head pieces to body pieces at waist edges at dotted seam lines shown. Join the completed pieces to each other at the edges marked with mouth lines. Machine-stitch along the mouth line four times with red thread. Draw thread ends through to wrong side and knot.

Tack gathered upper edges of sleeves to right sides of the striped body fabric at sides, starting at the waist seam, having raw edges level, hands pointing inwards and thumbs upwards.

Back piece

Cut and assemble pieces as for the front piece omitting mouth and leg line markings.

To assemble

Join front piece to back piece at remaining raw edges leaving a 14cm (5½in) gap in seam across top of head. Turn right side out and stuff firmly, then ladder-stitch the gap.

Legs

Cut two pairs of foot pieces from felt. Join them in pairs at centre front edges for a little of the seam only. For each leg cut a 15x19cm (6x7½in) strip of pink fabric. Join one long edge of each strip to the ankle edge of each foot. Now join remainder of foot seams and also short edges of legs. Trim seams round feet. Turn and stuff firmly to within 5cm (2in) of tops of legs, then stuff lightly. Stitch raw edges of each leg together, having leg seam at centre.

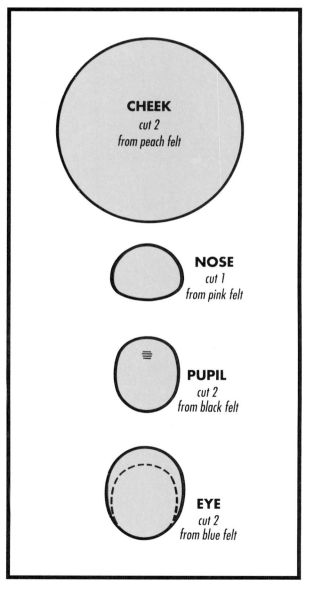

CHEEK
cut 2
from peach felt

NOSE
cut 1
from pink felt

PUPIL
cut 2
from black felt

EYE
cut 2
from blue felt

THE DAY THAT HUMPTY DUMPTY (NEARLY) WENT TO SEA

Humpty Dumpty was fed up. 'It's no fun at all falling off this horrible wall every day just to please the tourists,' he grumbled. 'I need a change. Today I will run away to sea!'

So off he went to the tailor's shop where he got fitted with a very natty sailor suit and a jaunty sailor hat. Then he set off walking on his own little legs to find the sea.

Humpty hadn't gone far when he came to the huge iron gates of the local park. There before him stretched acres of green grass and lots of tall trees. He took a deep breath. 'Fresh country air!' he sighed. 'And I think I can smell the sea, so it must be quite close by.' He carried on walking until he found himself beside the enormous lake in the middle of the park.

'I'm so pleased that the sea is calm today,' he said, looking down at the ducks paddling in the water, 'Because I wouldn't like to be sea sick!' But as there was not a single ship to be seen, he began to walk round the edge of the lake on his own little legs, until he came to the park band-stand. 'What a splendiferous building!' said Humpty. 'A pagoda, if I'm not mistaken, almost certainly built by the ancient Chinese people. Why, I must have travelled so far that I have walked all the way from my wall to China!'

Just then his tummy started to rumble because in the general excitement he had forgotten to eat his breakfast that morning. So off he went again on his own little legs to find something to eat. Imagine Humpty's delight when he saw an ice-cream van coming towards him. But he was amazed to read the sign above the van, which said 'Alberto's Best Italian Cornettos.'

'Why, I can't believe it!' Humpty cried excitedly. 'An Italian ice-cream seller. I must have walked all by myself on my own little legs all the way from my wall to China and now I am in Italy!' And he spoke to the ice-cream man in his best Italian. 'Beautiful day-o. May I have one-o cornetto please-o?' The ice-cream man, thinking that Humpty must be a foreign visitor, gave him an extra large helping.

Then Humpty set off again on his own little legs, calling to the ice-cream man, 'Cheerio-o Alberto, your cornettos are very nice-o!' He was really enjoying his ice-cream when suddenly a big shaggy dog came bounding out of the

Trouser Legs

Cut four trouser-leg pieces from striped fabric, placing pattern to fold each time as indicated. Join the pieces in pairs all round edges, leaving the ankle edges open. Turn right side out. Narrowly hem the ankle edges then sew on ric-rac. Push the legs inside trouser legs so that the upper edges of legs are level with the seamed top edges of trouser legs. Stitch across trousers through all thicknesses, 1cm (⅜in) away from the top edges. Sew top edges of trousers to marked lines on the front body pieces.

Face

Cut all the facial features from felt as indicated on patterns. Work a highlight on each black pupil with white thread as shown on pattern. Glue nose to face 3cm (1¼in) above mouth. Glue pupils to eyes then glue the eyes to face as illustrated, placing them 3cm (1¼in) apart. Sew the cheeks in place.

Waistband

Cut strip of ribbon to fit round the waist seam plus 1cm (⅜in). Fold it twice along the length to form a triple thickness, then press. Join the short ends. Stitch through the long edges. Put the waistband on Humpty with seam at centre front. Position the *upper* edge of waistband level with waist seam at front and *lower* edge of waistband level with waist seam at centre back. Glue waistband in place by pulling it away from the body a little at a time and dotting glue on the inside. Add a ribbon bow to centre front.

bushes. Humpty got such a fright that he dropped his ice-cream and ran off crying, 'Help! Help! A Humpty-eating lion is coming after me! I must have walked on my own little legs all the way from my wall, to China, to Italy and now I am in Africa!'

And he ran and ran, not looking where he was going, until he bumped into a man wearing a smart blue uniform and cap. Of course it was the park keeper, but Humpty thought he must be a policeman and probably a French policeman since his cap was a funny shape. So Humpty spoke to the park keeper in his best French. 'Bon . . . jour . . . Gen . . . darme,' he said getting his breath back. 'Avez-vous any idea where je can find un ship?'

The park keeper, thinking that Humpty must be a foreign visitor, replied in his best French. 'Bonjour Monsieur,' he said, 'Vous are quite out of puff! Avez-vous travelled far?'

'Oh kilometres and kilometres!' said Humpty. 'In fact, all the way from my wall, to China and Italy and Africa and now je find je am in France!'

'Oh non-non,' said the park keeper shaking his head. 'Vous are mistaken Monsieur; vous

are in Grande Bretagne!'

'Goodness Gracious!' said Humpty. 'Je must have run so fast that je have run right through France into Grande Bretagne!' Of course Humpty didn't know that Grande Bretagne was French for Great Britain.

And now, after all the walking and running, Humpty's own little legs were so tired that all he wanted to do was to get back home and sit upon his dear little wall. So the park keeper very kindly showed him the way back to the park gates.

Meanwhile, back at Humpty's wall, there was a very, very long queue of tourists. When he arrived, they all clapped and cheered and told him how pleased they were that he had not managed to find a ship and run off to sea. Humpty just laughed. 'Ships!' he exclaimed. 'Who needs ships? I have managed to walk right around the world and not even get my feet wet. And today I am *not* going to fall off my wall, so there! Instead I will tell you all about my wonderful and exciting adventures. And do you know, Humpty was so good at telling tall stories, that he never, ever had to fall off his wall again.

Hair

Cast on 110 sts and work the looped pattern as follows:

1st row: K 1; *insert right-hand needle K-wise into next st, place first 2 fingers of left hand at back of st, wind yarn anti-clockwise round needle and fingers 4 times, then round tip of right-hand needle only, draw through the 5 loops; repeat from * to last st; K 1.

Next row is the cast-off row, (cast off loosely): K 1; *K 5 together, pass first st on right-hand needle over second st thus casting it off; repeat from * to last st; K 1, then cast off last st. Join the row ends and lay hair aside.

Cap

Cut two 26cm (10¼in) diameter circles of plain fabric. Cut a 17cm (6¾in) diameter circle from centre of one and discard it. Join

the circles round the outer edges. Trim seam and leave cap wrong side out. Cut a 26cm (10¼in) diameter circle of wadding and place it on top of the whole cap circle. Oversew the outer edges together.

For cap band cut a 6x60cm (2⅜x23¾in) strip of plain fabric and iron on a same-sized strip of interfacing. Join the short ends. Bring the long raw edges together having right side outside, and tack, then press. Stitch the tacked raw edges to the inner raw edge of cap with right sides together and raw edges level. Turn cap right side out and sew ric-rac to the band. Place the lower edge of band over the cast-off edge of hair and stitch in place. Place the cap on Humpty as shown in the illustration. Sew it to the head through the hair strip just below the cap band.

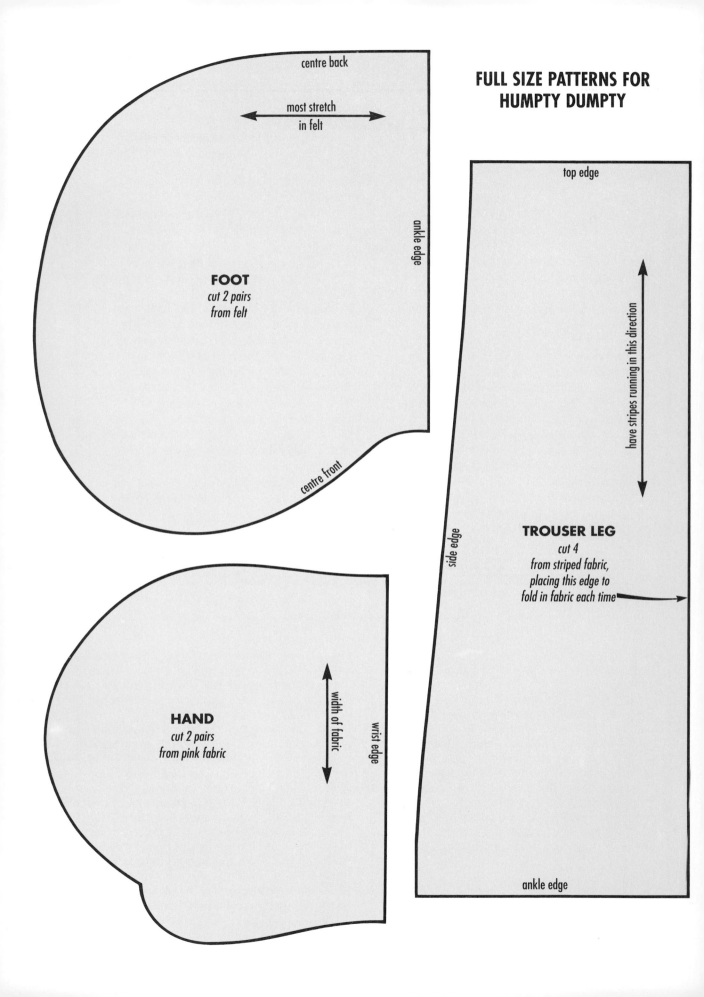

centre back

most stretch
in felt

ankle edge

FOOT
*cut 2 pairs
from felt*

centre front

**FULL SIZE PATTERNS FOR
HUMPTY DUMPTY**

top edge

have stripes running in this direction

side edge

TROUSER LEG
*cut 4
from striped fabric,
placing this edge to
fold in fabric each time*

HAND
*cut 2 pairs
from pink fabric*

width of fabric

wrist edge

ankle edge

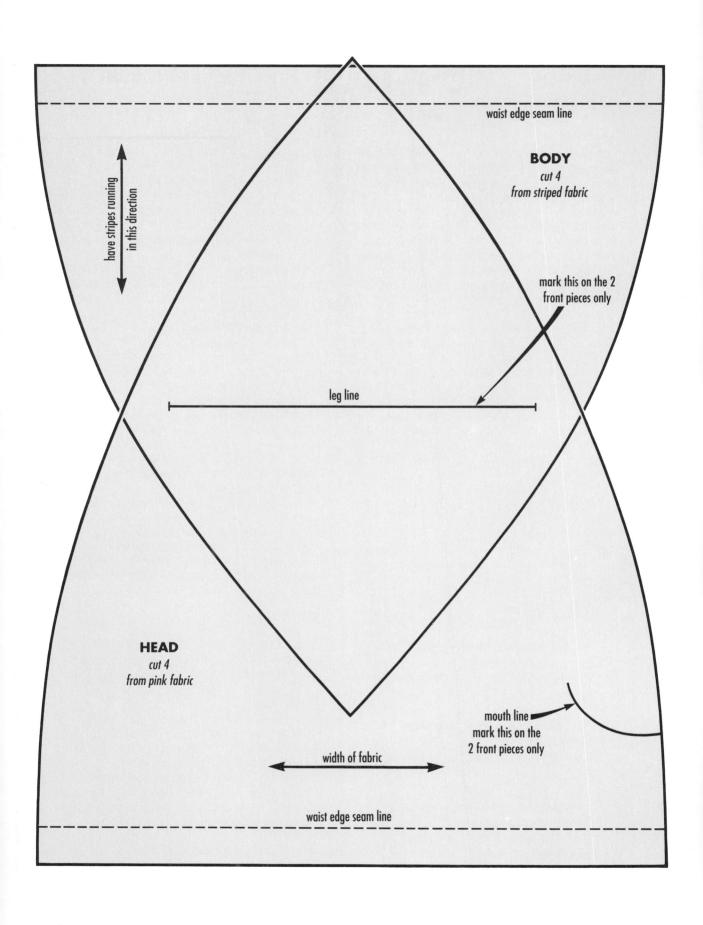

waist edge seam line

BODY
cut 4
from striped fabric

have stripes running
in this direction

mark this on the 2
front pieces only

leg line

HEAD
cut 4
from pink fabric

mouth line
mark this on the
2 front pieces only

width of fabric

waist edge seam line

Soft Tops

These cuddly toy vehicles are made from felt and interfacing. Each one is such fun to make and easy also, with two shaped pieces for the sides and a long straight strip for the gusset which joins the side pieces. The windows, wheels and other details are sewn in place after stuffing each vehicle. All the patterns are given full size and measurements are quoted for the circular wheel shapes. The van and caravan are about 16cm (6¼in) high and the cars just over 12cm (4¾in).

You will need: For each basic vehicle shape 25cm (¼yd) of 91cm (36in) wide felt and stuffing as specified in the individual instructions. For the finishing touches you will also need oddments of the following: medium-weight sew-in charcoal grey interfacing; superstretch white iron-on interfacing; firm sew-in white interfacing; black, grey, orange, yellow and red felt; a black and a blue permanent marker pen; black ball-point pen; adhesive.

TRAFFIC

The painter's van says 'Honk, honk, honk,
I've got no time to stop,
With paints and brushes stuffed inside
And ladders stacked on top.'

The little car says 'Beep, beep, beep,
I have to get away
And pull a yellow caravan
To go on holiday.'

The sporty car says 'Pip, pip, pip,
I'm off to take a run
Down to the beach then back again,
Should be a lot of fun.'

Notes: Trace all the patterns off the pages and mark on details. The side window and door pieces should be traced off the patterns given for the vehicle side pieces. Take care to cut out the vehicle side pieces with *width* of felt in direction shown. 5mm (¼in) seams are allowed when stitching the seams on the basic vehicles.

To achieve the effect of the 'glass' windows, proceed as follows. First iron a piece of the superstretch white interfacing onto a piece of the charcoal grey interfacing, following manufacturer's instructions for bonding. Noting that the *white* side is the right side when cutting out, cut out the required window shape. Colour a narrow strip all round the edge of the window, using the black pen. Now draw a few random diagonal lines across the window using the ball-point pen. Finally shade the window here and there with the blue pen. Blot all markings with a paper tissue, then iron the window with a clean tissue covering it. See the windows in illustration for this effect.

Use an iron to smooth out seams after the vehicles have been stuffed. Press all the window and door pieces etc after sewing them in place. See the illustrations when positioning the lights, number plates etc. Hand-sew all the details onto the stuffed shape using matching sewing threads.

THE VAN

You will need: Red felt; 250g (9oz) of stuffing; a 22cm (8¾in) length of narrow black elastic.

Basic Van
Cut two van side pieces from red felt. For the gusset, cut a 10x62cm (4x24½in) strip of red felt. Turn in the ends 1cm (⅜in) and catch down. Tack the long edges of gusset round the edges of side pieces, placing ends of gusset at point A. Stitch as tacked. Turn van right side out and stuff firmly, then ladder-stitch the ends of the gusset together.

Doors and windows
Cut one pair of side windows and sew in place. Cut one pair of side doors from red felt,

(Continued on page 74)

68

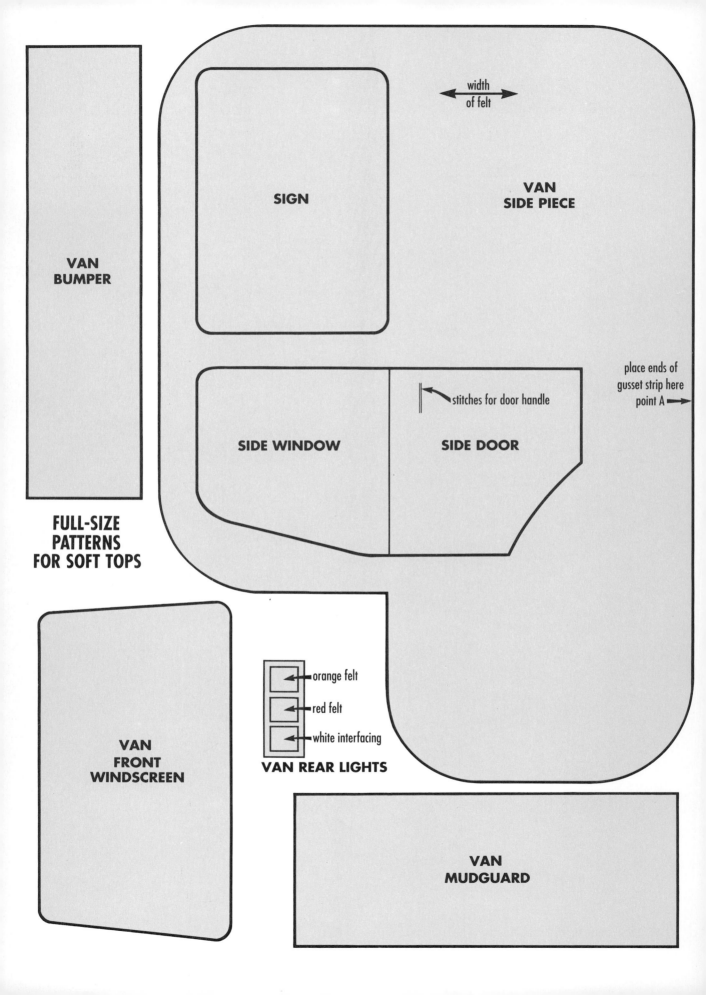

VAN BUMPER

SIGN

VAN
SIDE PIECE

width
of felt

place ends of
gusset strip here
point A →

stitches for door handle

SIDE WINDOW

SIDE DOOR

FULL-SIZE
PATTERNS
FOR SOFT TOPS

VAN
FRONT
WINDSCREEN

orange felt

red felt

white interfacing

VAN REAR LIGHTS

VAN
MUDGUARD

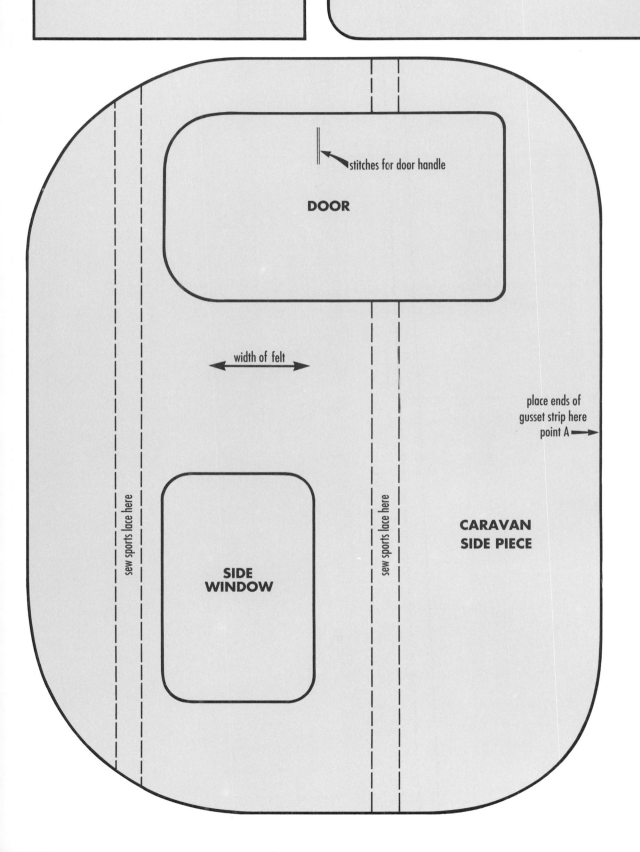

SPORTS CAR FRONT WINDSCREEN

CARAVAN FRONT AND BACK WINDOW

stitches for door handle

DOOR

width of felt

place ends of gusset strip here point A →

sew sports lace here

sew sports lace here

CARAVAN SIDE PIECE

SIDE WINDOW

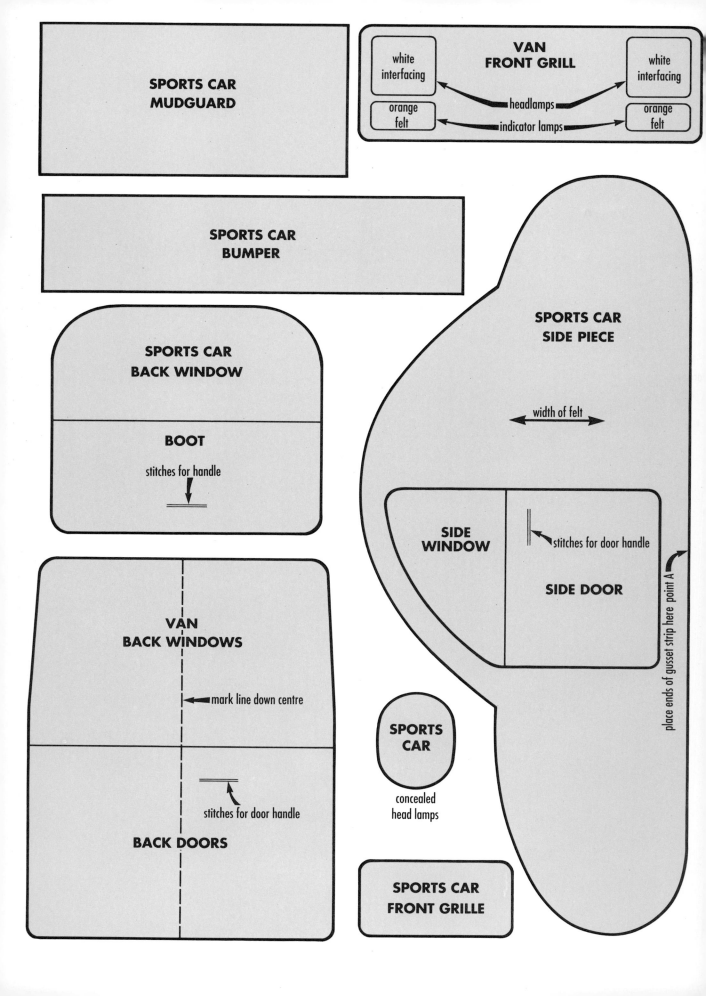

SPORTS CAR MUDGUARD

VAN FRONT GRILL

white interfacing

white interfacing

orange felt

orange felt

headlamps

indicator lamps

SPORTS CAR BUMPER

SPORTS CAR SIDE PIECE

width of felt

SPORTS CAR BACK WINDOW

BOOT

stitches for handle

SIDE WINDOW

stitches for door handle

SIDE DOOR

place ends of gusset strip here point A

VAN BACK WINDOWS

mark line down centre

stitches for door handle

BACK DOORS

SPORTS CAR

concealed head lamps

SPORTS CAR FRONT GRILLE

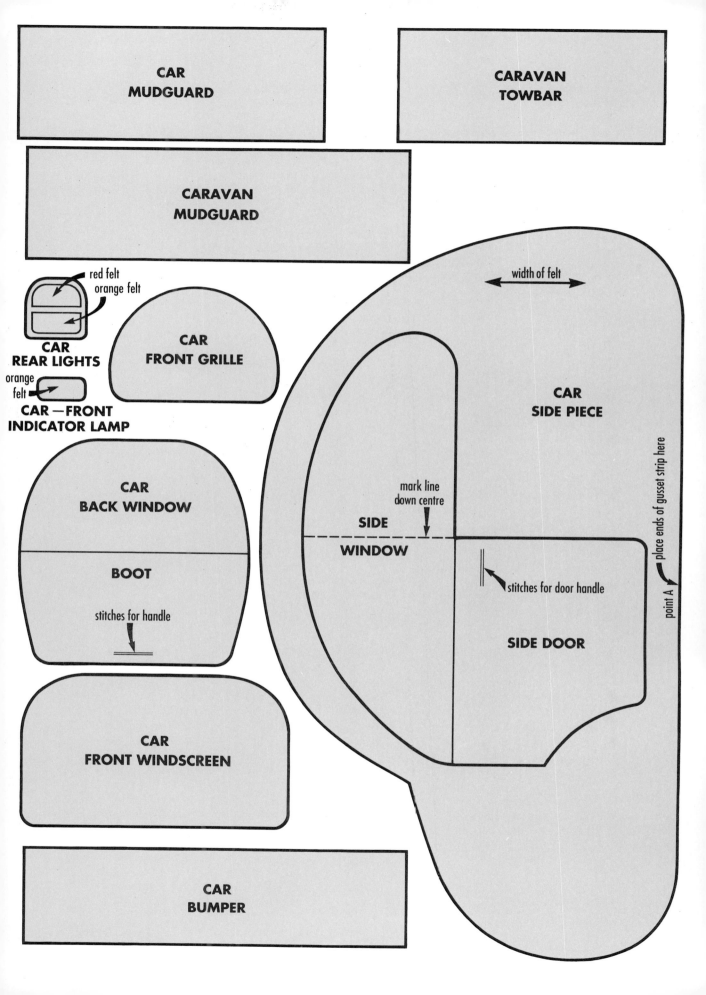

CAR
MUDGUARD

CARAVAN
TOWBAR

CARAVAN
MUDGUARD

red felt
orange felt

CAR
REAR LIGHTS

orange
felt

CAR — FRONT
INDICATOR LAMP

CAR
FRONT GRILLE

width of felt

CAR
SIDE PIECE

CAR
BACK WINDOW

BOOT

stitches for handle

mark line
down centre

SIDE
WINDOW

stitches for door handle

SIDE DOOR

point A

place ends of gusset strip here

CAR
FRONT WINDSCREEN

CAR
BUMPER

mark round the edges with black marker pen except for the upper edges. Work black stitches for handle. Sew the doors in place. Cut front windscreen, back window and back red felt door pieces, mark them as before, then sew them in place.

Cut two sign pieces from two layers of heavy white interfacing glued together. Mark on details as illustrated (or details of your choice), then sew in place.

Front grill

Cut this from the window fabric but have the charcoal grey side as the right side. Mark round the edges and draw horizontal lines across. Cut the headlamps from white as for the sign, and the indicators from orange felt. Sew them to grill, then sew grill in place.

Bumpers

Cut two from black felt. Oversew the long edges of each one together. Press the bumpers with the oversewn seams at back. Sew to front and back of van below the grill and the back door.

For number plates, cut a 1x3cm (⅜x1¼in) strip from two layers of firm white interfacing glued together and also one from yellow felt. Mark on the registration number. Sew the white plate to centre front and yellow plate to centre back of bumpers.

Rear lights

Cut two by outline of pattern from black felt. Glue on smaller coloured squares of felt as shown on the pattern. Sew rear lights in place vertically on either side of the back doors.

Wheels

Cut four 12cm (4¾in) diameter circles of black felt. Gather round the edge of each one and stuff lightly. Pull up the gathers, leaving a finger-sized hole, then fasten off. Continue stuffing using scissor points to push stuffing well in, towards the rim of wheel all round.

For centre hub of each wheel, cut a 3cm (1¼in) diameter circle from two layers of grey felt glued together. Mark the centre and dots around centre as illustrated. Sew the hub to wheel, covering the hole in wheel. Pin wheels to van as illustrated, then ladder-stitch them to van where they touch.

Cut four mudguards from red felt and sew and press in the same way as for the bumpers. Place a bumper over each wheel. Round off the outer corners of bumper. Oversew these cut edges together. Sew the mudguards to sides of van, then to the wheels.

Roof rack

Cut the elastic in two pieces. Turn in the ends and sew them to seams on roof as illustrated.

Ladder

Cut a 3x24cm (1¼x9½in) strip of grey felt. Fold the strip in three along the length, press, then stitch the long edges. Cut the strip into six equal pieces for the steps. For the ladder side pieces, cut two 3x20cm (1¼x8in) strips of grey felt. Fold and press as for the steps. Open up the folds. Stick one long edge of each strip down. Now glue the ends of the steps to folded down edges of strips spacing them 1.5cm (⅝in) apart. Glue down the remaining long edges of the ladder side pieces enclosing ends of steps. Trim ends of ladder side pieces, then stitch all round edges of the side pieces.

THE CAR

You will need: Blue felt and 170g (6oz) of stuffing.
Make as for Van using the Car patterns and the following measurements for the other pieces: Gusset strip, 8x51cm (3¼x20in); for headlamps, two 1.5cm (⅝in) diameter circles of firm white interfacing; for wheels, four 10cm (4in) diameter black felt circles.

THE CARAVAN

You will need: Yellow felt; 280g (10oz) stuffing; 1.15m (46in) length of fancy sports shoelace; two snap fasteners.

Make as for Van using Caravan patterns and a 10x61cm (4x24in) gusset strip. Make two wheels as for Van. After sewing on the door, sew on the sports shoelace at positions shown. Sew *two* windows to the Caravan on the side opposite door. Make rear lights and number plate as for the Car. Cut the tow-bar from black felt, fold in three along length and stitch the long edges. Attach to Car and to Caravan with snap fasteners.

THE SPORTS CAR

You will need: Pink felt and 140g (5oz) stuffing.

Make as for the Van using Sports Car patterns and a 9x48cm (3½x19in) gusset strip. Use pink felt for the concealed headlamps, marking with black pen round edges. Make the rear lights as for Van, sewing them in place horizontally above the back bumper.

Sleeping Beauty and the Prince

Both Sleeping Beauty and the Prince can be made from the same basic doll patterns. Beauty is a reversible doll – she has a sleepy face on one side and a wideawake face on the other. The head-dress, sewn across the top of her head, covers each face in turn. The dolls are about 48cm (19in) high. Beauty has an everyday gown plus a wedding dress, while the Prince's clothes are sewn in place except for the sleeveless jacket.

SLEEPING BEAUTY

For the doll you will need: 50cm (⅝yd) of 91cm (36in) wide pink cotton fabric; a 25g (1oz) ball of double-knitting yarn for the hair; 250g (½lb) of stuffing; scrap of black felt for the eyes; small pieces of felt and trimming for the shoes; a red pencil; adhesive.

For the everyday gown you will need: 50cm (⅝yd) of 91cm (36in) wide printed fabric; short length of lace trimming; small pieces of fur fabric; 60cm (¾yd) of narrow ribbon; three buttons, or hooks and eyes.

For the wedding dress you will need: White fabric (the same amounts of fabric and fur fabric as for the gown); 1.40m (1½yd) of fancy braid; three buttons, or hooks and eyes.

For the head-dress you will need: A 45cm (18in) diameter semi-circle of fabric to tone with the everyday gown and a 25cm (9¾in) length of braid; a 45cm (18in) diameter semi-circle of the same fabric as the wedding dress and a 25cm (9¾in) length of fancy trimming.

Notes: 5mm (¼in) seams are allowed on all pieces unless otherwise stated. Cut the head gusset piece on the *bias* of the fabric but cut all other pieces on the straight grain.

Patterns: The patterns are printed full size for tracing off the page. The doll body and head pattern and the head gusset are too large to print in one piece on the page, so trace off as follows. For the gusset, trace onto folded paper, as indicated, cut out and open

up to give a full-size pattern. Trace the two doll body and head pieces onto folded paper in the same way. Cut them out and open up, then join them at the neck lines X–Y.

Beauty's leg pattern is a rectangle – cut a 7.5x25cm (3x9¾in) strip of paper and round off the corners at one end, for the foot. Mark the pattern 'Beauty Leg' and use as directed in the instructions. Trace off all other patterns and mark on details.

Body and head

Cut two body and head pieces and on the wrong side of each one, mark the neck dart. On the right side of both pieces mark the

SLEEPING BEAUTY

Now I'm sure you must have heard the tale of the pretty young princess called Sleeping Beauty, who dozed off for a hundred years. Well, I'm going to tell it again as there were some facts which didn't emerge at the time.

You probably remember that when the princess was born, her mum and dad gave a big party. They invited some very important people, some not-so-important people and all the fairies, witches and magic people because they didn't want to be turned into toads or anything.

But they quite forgot to invite a particularly bad-tempered witch called Grizelda. Well actually, *they* didn't forget – the postman did. The witch lived a long way off and the postman was just going home to tea, so he put the invitation behind the mantelpiece clock and forgot all about it. It's probably still there!

Anyway, Grizelda was so cross at being left out, that she gatecrashed the party and put a horrible curse on the baby, saying that when the princess grew up she would prick her finger on a contraption called a spinning wheel and die – straight away!

Luckily, a very nice fairy managed to change the curse to a spell and shortened it to a one-hundred-year snooze. So that was a bit better at least. But there was no stopping fate altogether, so the princess did grow up, did prick her finger and did fall asleep – for one hundred years. Now it wouldn't have been so bad if all the servants could have stayed awake to keep the place tidy, but the spell was so strong that it affected everybody – dogs, cats, mice and people. The only creatures which didn't zonk out were the spiders, because it seems that witches are quite fond of creepy-crawlies, aren't they?

And now you must be thinking that I'm going to go on about the handsome prince turning up after one hundred years to break the spell. Not so!

About 51¾ years later, a not-so-handsome prince came galloping past. Well, to tell you the truth, he was actually downright ugly, with a wart on his nose, slightly crossed eyes and a bad case of knobbly knees which looked dreadful when he wore tights (which was all the time). Besides being ugly, the prince was also a stickler for tidiness and dust-free surfaces. He was the kind of prince who hoovered again after the cleaning lady had just left.

He was also a very nosey chap, and seeing the Palace completely overgrown he charged through the bushes and straight in at the front door without even bothering to knock. Did I mention that he didn't have any manners either?

When the ugly prince saw the 51¾ years of dust in the place he came over all funny, but he still couldn't resist poking his nose into every corner, because as I have already said, he was a proper nosey-parker.

Eventually, he got to the princess's bedroom, fell in love at first sight and there and then decided to kiss her quick and carry her off.

Well now, what a disaster *that* would have been. The beautiful princess married to an ugly knock-kneed prince with a wart on his nose; it's never heard of in fairy-tale happy endings, is it? Luckily, it was not to be.

Remember the wide-awake spiders . . .? Well the ugly prince simply couldn't *stand* spiders, in fact he had a *phobia* about them, which means that he couldn't stand them even worse!

So, just as he was about to give the princess a smacking great kiss, a large black spider crawled from under the bed clothes . . . and winked at him! 'Hurray for the spider!' I hear you cheer! The prince shot off as though there were trillions of tarantulas after him and of course was never seen again.

However, I'm sorry that the story can't end just yet, because the princess had to carry on snoring for another 48¼ years before the really handsome prince could come along to wake her up and marry her!

mouth, nose and eyebrow lines. On *one* of the pieces mark the solid eyelid and eyelash lines for the sleeping face. On the other piece, mark the dotted outline and eyelashes for the wide-awake eyes. On both heads, mark points D lightly on right side. Stitch the neck darts, then trim off folded edges of the darts. Cut one head gusset on the bias. Sew the long edges to the head, matching points A and B.

Now join the body pieces from points A to C, taking care not to catch in the ends of the gusset. Turn body and head right side out and stuff firmly. Turn in lower edges 1cm (⅜in) and slip-stitch to close.

Work both sets of facial lines in small stitches using sewing threads. Use red for the mouths and black for the eyelashes, eyebrows and the eyelid lines. Mark the nose line and colour the cheeks with red pencil.

Cut the wide-awake eyes from black felt, the same size as the dotted lines. Work a small highlight on each one, using white thread. Glue the eyes in place.

Hair

Wind the yarn into a hank measuring about 80cm (32in) across. Cut through both looped ends of the hank. Machine-stitch through the centre of the yarn strands, spreading them out to measure about 7cm (2¾in) in width.

Sew this centre parting stitching line to top of head between points D on each head. Gather the yarn strands smoothly to each side of the head and sew to the position shown on the gusset pattern. Plait the strands, then tie a length of yarn round the end of each plait to secure.

Legs

Cut two pairs of leg pieces and join them in pairs at long edges and round feet, leaving short straight upper edges open. Trim seams around feet, turn right side out and stuff to within 2cm (¾in) of tops. Turn in the top edges 1cm (⅜in) and slip-stitch to close, then sew legs to lower edge of the body.

Arms

Cut two pairs of arm pieces and make them as for the legs stuffing to within 5cm (2in) of the top edges. Turn in the top edges 1cm (⅜in) and slip-stitch to close pulling the stitches tightly to gather. Sew the arms to sides of the body, 1.5cm (⅝in) down from the neck.

Shoes

To make the shoes, cut the lower 5cm (2in) off the leg pattern. Cut four pieces from felt. Join them round the curved edges, leaving the upper edges open. Trim seams and turn right side out.

Put the felt shoes on the ends of the legs and sew the top edges in place. Sew trimming round these top edges.

Everyday gown

Cut the bodice pieces as stated on the patterns. Join the front to backs at side and shoulder edges. Cut and make another bodice piece, for the lining. Join the bodice to the lining round the neck and back edges. Clip curves and corners, turn right side out and press. Tack the armhole edges of bodice and lining together.

Cut two sleeves as stated on the pattern. Run a gathering thread along each armhole edge between the dots on the pattern. Join the underarm edges of each sleeve. Turn sleeves right side out and join armhole edges to the bodice armholes, pulling up gathers in sleeves to fit. Neaten the raw armhole edges.

Cut two fur cuffs, using the lower portion of the sleeve pattern as shown. Join the under-arm edges of cuff pieces. Join lower edges of cuffs to lower edges of sleeves, with right side of cuffs against *wrong* side of sleeves and raw edges level. Now turn the cuffs right back over right side of the sleeves. Turn in cuff raw

edges and slip-stitch them to the sleeves.

For the dress skirt, cut a 30x70cm (11¾x28in) strip of fabric. Join the short edges, taking a 2cm (¾in) seam and leaving 8cm (3in) open at top of seam for back skirt opening. Press seam to one side and neaten the raw edges of the opening.

Gather the top edge of the skirt to fit the lower edge of the bodice, then sew it in place leaving the lining free. Turn in lower edge of the bodice lining and slip-stitch it over the seam. Sew a 4cm (1½in) wide strip of fur fabric to the lower edge of the skirt in the same way as for the sleeve cuffs. Sew the short length of lace trimming round the neck. Tie the ribbon in a bow with long ends. Sew it to the bodice front at the waist. Sew on the buttons and make buttonholes in the bodice back edges, or sew on hooks and eyes to fasten.

Wedding dress

Follow the instructions for the other gown. Sew the fancy braid round the neck edge. Sew braid also to the fur fabric trimming at the upper edges of the cuffs and also the fur fabric at the hem.

Head-dress

Join the two semi-circles of fabric round the edges, leaving a gap in the seam. Turn right side out and press, then slip-stitch the gap.

Pin the centre of the straight edge to the centre top of the head gusset, with the wedding-dress fabric uppermost and the wide-awake face exposed. Continue pinning the straight edge to the head gusset until you reach the top of the plaited hair at each side of the head. Sew the straight edge in place, taking the stitches through the hair and into the head gusset fabric. Sew the fancy trimming to the head, just in front of the straight edge of the head-dress. Flip the head-dress over and sew the length of braid to the other side of the head in the same way.

THE PRINCE

For the doll you will need: 50cm (⅝yd) of 91cm (36in) wide pink cotton fabric; a 25g (1oz) ball of double-knitting yarn for the hair; 250g (½lb) of stuffing; scrap of black felt for the eyes; small piece of striped fabric for the upper legs; small amount of felt for the boots; a red pencil; adhesive.

For the cap you will need: a 24cm (9½in) diameter circle of fabric or felt and a few feathers.

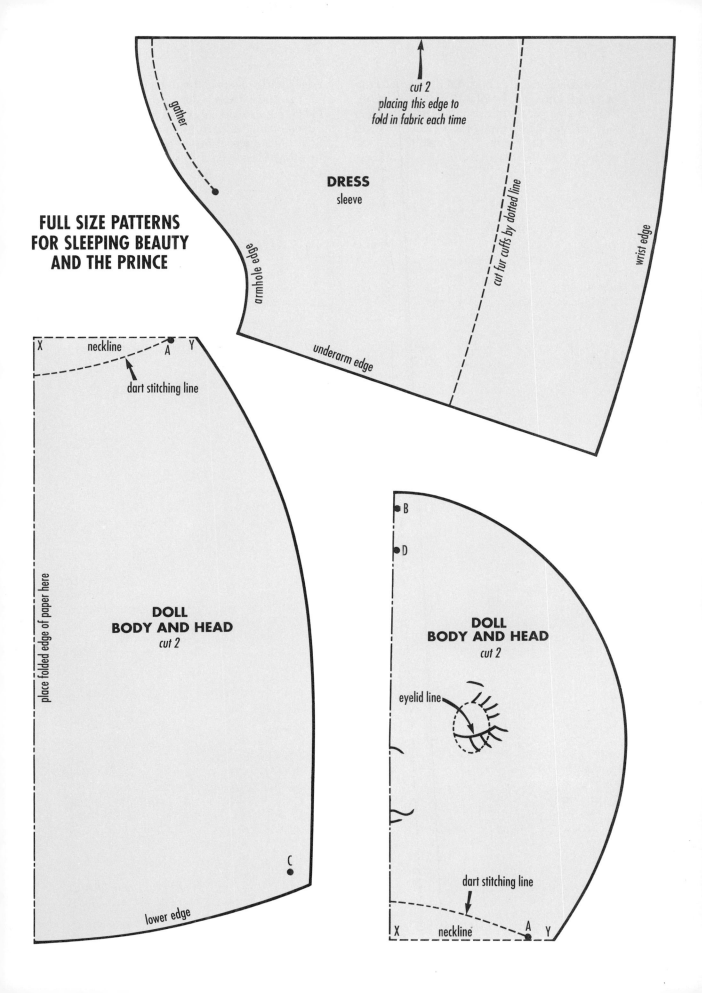

FULL SIZE PATTERNS FOR SLEEPING BEAUTY AND THE PRINCE

DRESS
sleeve

*cut 2
placing this edge to
fold in fabric each time*

gather

armhole edge

cut fur cuffs by dotted line

wrist edge

underarm edge

dart stitching line

X neckline A Y

place folded edge of paper here

**DOLL
BODY AND HEAD**
cut 2

C

lower edge

B

D

**DOLL
BODY AND HEAD**
cut 2

eyelid line

dart stitching line

X neckline A Y

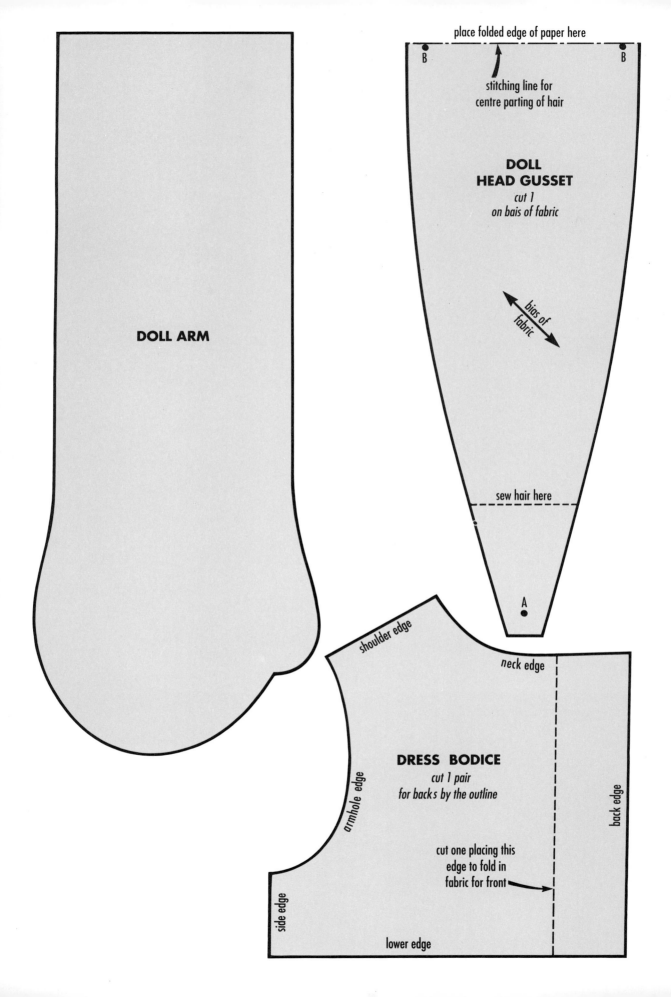

DOLL ARM

place folded edge of paper here

B ●   B ●

stitching line for
centre parting of hair

**DOLL
HEAD GUSSET**
*cut 1
on bais of fabric*

bias of
fabric

sew hair here

A ●

shoulder edge

neck edge

DRESS BODICE
*cut 1 pair
for backs by the outline*

armhole edge

back edge

cut one placing this
edge to fold in
fabric for front

side edge

lower edge

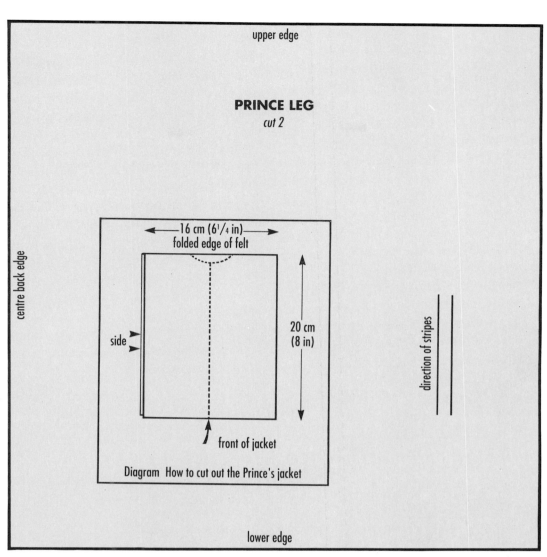

upper edge

PRINCE LEG
cut 2

centre back edge

16 cm (6¼ in)
folded edge of felt

20 cm
(8 in)

side

front of jacket

Diagram How to cut out the Prince's jacket

direction of stripes

lower edge

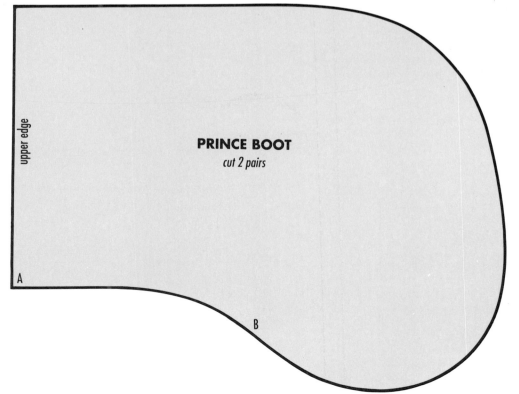

upper edge

PRINCE BOOT
cut 2 pairs

A

B

For the shirt you will need: 20cm (¼yd) of 91cm (36in) wide fabric and 90cm (1yd) of narrow braid.

For the jacket you will need: a 16x40cm (6¼x16in) strip of felt and 1.30m (1⅜yd) of fancy braid.

Body and head
Make the body and head as for Sleeping Beauty, but work the wide-awake face only.

Arms
Make the arms as for Sleeping Beauty, but lay them aside until later.

Hair
For the hair, first make the forehead fringe as follows. Wind the yarn round the width of a 6x10cm (2½x4in) strip of thin card, to cover the card. Machine-stitch through the loops at one long edge. Slip the loops off the card, tearing the card away from the stitching, if necessary. Sew the stitched edge of the fringe centrally across the gusset seam, above the face.

For the second portion of the hair, wind the yarn about 40 times round a 24cm (9½in) length of card. Slip the yarn off the card and sew the centre of this hank along the centre parting line of the gusset. Take the looped ends of the yarn and catch them all down together to the gusset at each side of the face.

Make another hank of yarn in the same way, round an 18cm (7in) length of card. Sew the centre just behind the first hank. Now take the looped ends down the back of the head and catch them to the head just above the neck, to cover the head completely.

Legs
Cut two leg pieces from striped fabric using the pattern. Cut two pairs of boot pieces from felt. Join the boot pieces in pairs from A to B. Join the upper edges of boot pieces to the lower edges of legs, right sides together and raw edges level. Now join remainder of boot seams and centre-back edges of legs, leaving upper edges open. Trim seams, turn legs right side out, stuff and finish as for Sleeping Beauty.

For the top cuff on each boot, cut a 5cm (2in) wide strip of felt, long enough to go round the boot plus a little extra for a seam. Join the short edges of each strip for 3cm (1¼in) only, leaving remainder open. Cut

2cm (¾in) long snips along this edge at regular intervals.

Slip the boot tops on the legs, with seams at centre back and the snipped edges pointing upwards. Sew the unsnipped edges to tops of the boots. Turn the boot tops down, then sew the legs to the body as for Sleeping Beauty.

Cap
Turn in the edge of the fabric or felt circle 5mm (¼in) and run round a gathering thread. Pull up the gathers to fit the head, then fasten off. Sew the gathered edge to head. Sew the feathers to front of the cap as shown in the illustration.

Shirt
For the body of the shirt cut a 20x34cm (8x13½in) strip of fabric. Join the short edges. Turn right side out. Narrowly hem one remaining raw edge and sew on braid. Turn in the other raw edge 2cm (¾in) and press. Run a gathering thread round, 1cm (⅜in) away from the pressed fold. Slip the shirt on the doll, pull up the gathers tightly around the neck, then fasten off. Space out the gathers evenly, then sew them to the neck. Sew a strip of braid round the gathers.

For each sleeve, cut an 18x20cm (7x8in) strip of fabric. Join the short edges of each strip, then turn right side out. Turn in one remaining raw edge 2cm (¾in) and press. Gather these edges around the arms at the wrists and sew on braid as for the neck. Turn in the remaining raw edge 1cm (⅜in) and slip-stitch to close, pulling stitches to gather and at the same time catching the top of the arms in the stitches.

Now sew the arms to the doll at each side taking your stitches through the shirt fabric and into the body.

Jacket
Fold the felt strip in half and cut one half open for the centre front as shown in the diagram. Cut out the neckline as shown, using the Sleeping Beauty front bodice pattern neckline as a guide. Trim another 5mm (¼in) off the neckline. Round off the upper and lower corners of the jacket front edges. Join the side edges of the jacket, oversewing them together and leaving 7cm (2¾in) open at the tops for the armholes. Turn the jacket right side out. Sew the fancy braid round the jacket edges and the armhole edges also.

Zoo rug

Here is a softly padded playrug which brings all the fun of a visit to the zoo into your home. The finished rug measures about 90cm (36in) in diameter. There are also full-size patterns for nine different tiny animals – all made from stretchy towelling socks, plus some little children visitors. The zoo rhyme can be enjoyed by all the family, with the children asking the question 'Why not?' to each zoo rule.

You will need: 1.90m (2yd) of 91cm (36in) wide fabric (such as inexpensive non-woven curtaining); oddments of the following: blue fabric for water, striped fabric for barred edges of enclosures, fawn, brown or grey tweedy fabrics for rocky islands and walls etc, green towelling or other fabric, and fur fabric for vegetation; stuffing; brown permanent marker pen; adhesive (optional, but useful for holding small pieces in place before sewing).

ZOO RULES – OK?

Please do not hand a
bun to the panda.
 'Why not?'
Because he's on a diet.

Please do not pat
the tiger cat.
 'Why not?'
Because pats are only for pets.

Please do not make
the elephant shake.
 'Why not?'
Because he might fall over and squash you flat.

Please do not kneel
beside the seal.
 'Why not?'
Because he'll probably stuff a fish in your mouth.

Please do not smack
the polar bear's back.
 'Why not?'
Because he'll turn right around and give you what for.

Please do not repose
on the hippo's toes.
 'Why not?'
Because he might jump on yours and he's bigger than you.

Please do not stare
at the big brown bear.
 'Why not?'
Because he will think you are very rude and never speak to you again.

Please do not tread
on the crocodile's head.
 'Why not?'
Because he has about a million very sharp teeth and knows how to use them.

Please do not squeeze
the lion's knees.
 'Why not?'
Because he'll almost certainly gobble you up and you won't be home in time for tea and it will serve you jolly well right for asking so many questions!
THAT'S WHY NOT!

Notes: The basic rug is made from two circles of fabric and you can use any available pieces of firm fabric such as an old blanket or curtaining since this fabric will not be visible on the finished rug. However, quantities are given above, in case this fabric has to be purchased. 1cm (⅜in) seams are allowed on all pieces unless otherwise stated.

To draw the pattern for the circle

You need a 50cm (20in) square of brown wrapping paper for the pattern plus string, a pin and a pencil. Knot one end of the string and push the pin through it and into one corner of the square. Knot the string round the pencil point 45cm (18in) away from the pin.

Now keeping string taut draw the quarter circle onto paper as shown in Diagram 1. Cut out the pattern. Now mark another quarter circle on pattern in same way, 18cm (7in) away from the pin.

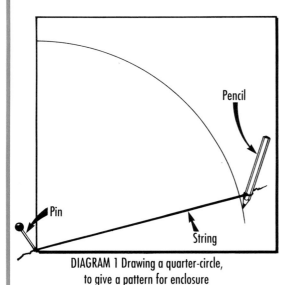

DIAGRAM 1 Drawing a quarter-circle, to give a pattern for enclosure

THE RUG

To make the basic rug

Mark one piece of basic rug fabric into quarters. Pin the quarter-circle pattern to each quarter in turn and cut out fabric level with outer curved edge. Fold the pattern in half as shown in Diagram 2 (see p 86), then use this pattern to mark four more lines radiating from centre of circle, thus dividing it into eight sections.

Now pin the circle of fabric onto remaining piece of rug fabric and cut it out level with

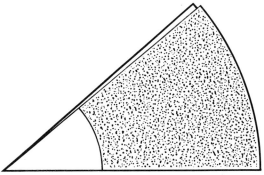

DIAGRAM 2 Showing this pattern folded in half, to form one-eighth of a circle. Use the shaded portion as a pattern for each enclosure

edge of circle. Tack circles of fabric together round the edges and along the marked section lines.

Trim the pattern along the inner marked curve and use the shaded piece shown in Diagram 2 as a pattern for each of the enclosures, adding 1cm (⅜in) to the straight side edges for the seam allowance.

Grassy enclosures (for lions, pandas, brown bears and tigers)

Using the enclosure pattern cut four pieces from green towelling or fabric. Cut a small irregular hole about 6cm (2¼in) across in each piece for the water hole. Clip at right angles round raw edges of the holes then turn in and tack these raw edges.

Place each green fabric piece in position on the rug leaving an enclosure space between each one for the water enclosures. Slip pieces of blue fabric underneath each cut-out water hole. Now tack the green fabric pieces in place round the edges and also sew to rug round edges of water holes.

Water enclosures (for hippos, crocodiles, seals and polar bears)

Cut four pieces from blue fabric as for the grassy enclosures. Turn in and press seam allowances at side edges. Tack pieces in position on rug overlapping side edges of the blue fabric pieces over side raw edges of green fabric. Sew side edges of each blue piece in place.

Path

Cut a 44cm (17¼in) diameter circle of light fawn or grey fabric and turn in and tack raw edge. Sew circle to centre of rug.

Elephant enclosure

Cut a 30cm (11¾in) diameter circle of fawn fabric. Cut and make a water hole as for the other enclosures. Cut a 10cm (4in) wide strip of tweedy fabric suitable for the wall, long enough to go round edge of circle plus seam allowance. Join ends of strip. Stitch one long edge of strip round edge of fabric circle on the right side, with raw edges level. Now turn in the remaining long edge and slip-stitch it over seam line, at the same time stuffing wall as you go. Place enclosure on the rug at centre of the path circle putting a piece of blue fabric under the cut-out water hole. Sew in place just under the wall and also sew round edge of water hole. Use the marker pen to draw paving stones on the path as shown in the illustration.

Outer wall

Make and sew in place round the outer edge of the rug in same way as for the elephant enclosure wall, joining strips of fabric to form an approximate length of 3.20m (3½yd).

Water enclosure walls (make four)

For each one cut a 10x66cm (4x26in) strip of the wall fabric. Turn in seam allowance at the ends and also one long edge and tack. Stitch the seam line at remaining long raw edge all round edge of the water. Now slip-stitch the remaining long edge to edge of green fabric, at the same time stuffing the wall as you go. Finally slip-stitch the short ends of wall to the outer wall of the rug.

Grassy enclosure bars (make four)

For each one cut a 10x17cm (4x6¾in) strip of striped fabric. Make and sew in place in the same way as for water enclosure walls, then sew ends of bars to walls.

Islands and rocks

For largest islands in the centre of water enclosures first cut a 16x24cm (6¼x9½in) rectangle of suitable fabric and if desired, shade here and there with marker pen. Cut edges into irregular shapes and then gather all round the edge of the piece. Pull up gathers to turn in the raw edge, then stuff lightly. Sew the turned-in edges to the water, then give the island more shape by taking stab stitches through it to the back of the rug, pulling thread tightly and fastening off. Make smaller rocks in a similar way for the grassy enclosures.

Bushes and foliage

Cut small irregular pieces of fur fabric and make and sew in place here and there as for the islands and rocks.

THE ANIMALS

You will need: Stretch towelling socks in colours illustrated; stuffing; Plasticine; scraps of felt and fur fabric; black permanent marker pen; small black beads 3mm (⅛in) to 5mm (¼in) in diameter (3mm for smallest animals, 5mm for elephants) or, if toys are for a very young child, use small felt circles instead; adhesive.

Notes: the smallest animals are about 8cm (3¼in) in length.

First, cut off and discard the elasticated strip at top of each sock (this bit is unsuitable). Cut open the sock down centre back and underneath the foot. Each animal is made from one colour of sock except for Panda, where you will need a black and a white sock. You can get three or four animals from one sock.

Trace the patterns off page onto thin paper and mark on all details. When cutting pieces from terry sock fabric, take care to have *arrows* on pattern pieces running *parallel with the length* of sock and following smooth stroke of the terry fabric (this can be up or down sock). Gather the pieces 3mm (⅛in) away from raw edges. Seams are also this size unless otherwise stated. All animals are made with right side of sock fabric as right side of animal except for the seal where wrong side of fabric is used for outside.

Before cutting out tiny felt pieces, spread back of felt with adhesive and work into felt with fingers. Leave to dry, then press. Cut felt ears to match body fabric except where otherwise stated.

Hippo

Pin body pattern to sock with length of pattern going along length of sock as indicated. Cut out body. Run a double gathering thread all round edge of body and pull up gathers a little. Now roll four balls of Plasticine about the size of a large pea. Stuff body, then tuck a ball of Plasticine into each gathered corner of body. Pull up gathers as tightly as possible, then fasten off. Work a few large oversewing stitches between the legs from front to back of body, then from side to side, pulling thread tightly to close the gathers completely.

Cut hippo head from sock fabric. Gather round the edge and stuff, then pull up gathers tightly and fasten off. Sew on beads for eyes as illustrated, taking sewing thread through from gathered back of head to face and back again.

Cut the ears and nostrils from pink felt. Mark a black dot at centre of each nostril. Glue nostrils in place then sew ears to top of head. Pin gathered back of head to front of body, turning head to one side, then ladder-stitch to body as pinned.

Cut tail from sock fabric and oversew side edges together, right side outside, pulling thread tightly. Sew short raw edge to back of hippo.

Tiger

Make body as for Hippo. Using black marker pen, mark stripes on body as shown in the illustration. Cut tiger head and make as for Hippo. Add eyes and ears as for Hippo. Cut nose from brown felt and colour shaded portion with pen. Glue nose in place. Using black thread work a straight line down from nose with a W at end of it for mouth. Make black markings on head as illustrated. Sew head to body, then make and add tail as for Hippo. Mark stripes across the tail.

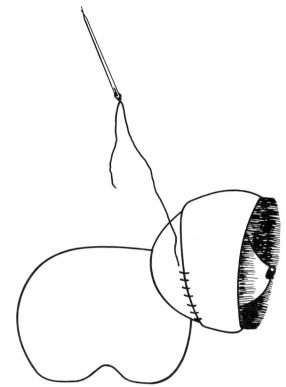

DIAGRAM 3 Sewing the mane to lion's head

Lion

Make body as for Hippo. Make head and add eyes as for Polar Bear using Lion head pattern. Cut nose from brown felt and stick in place.

Cut mane piece from fur fabric with smooth stroke of fur pile in direction of arrow shown on pattern. Oversew short edges of the strip together. Pin long straight edge of mane round face with right side of mane against face and short ends under chin (see Diagram 3). Slip-stitch long edge in place, then turn mane back over head. Cut lion's ears from felt and sew to mane just behind the long straight edge.

Cut tail from sock fabric, make and sew in place as for Hippo. Tie a strand of thread tightly round the tail, 1cm (⅜in) from the end.

Panda

Using black sock fabric, make body as for Hippo. Cut the back stripe piece from white sock fabric, turn in and tack raw edges loosely. Pin, then sew to back of body having the back point between back legs and side points between front and back legs.

Cut panda head from white sock and make as for Hippo. Cut eye patches, nose and ears from black felt. Work a few white stitches on

each eye patch piece as shown on pattern, then stick in place. Stick nose in place and sew ears to top of head. Sew head to body as for Hippo.

Polar bear

Make body as for Hippo. Cut one pair of polar bear head pieces and back-stitch them together leaving back edges open. Turn right side out and gather round raw edge. Stuff head, pull up gathers and fasten off. Add eyes and ears as for Hippo, then sew head to body. Cut nose from brown felt and stick in place.

Brown bear

Make exactly as for Polar Bear but use the Brown Bear ear pattern.

Elephant

Make body as for Hippo using the larger body pattern and larger balls of Plasticine. Make head, sew on eyes and sew head in place as for Polar Bear using elephant head pattern.

Cut two pairs of ears from sock fabric. Oversew them together round edges leaving the inner edges open. Turn right side out and oversew inner edges together. Sew ears to sides of head. Make elephant's tail and sew in place in same way as for Lion.

Seal

Use the inside of sock fabric as the right side. Cut one pair of body pieces. Back-stitch them together round edges leaving lower edges open. Turn right side out and stuff. Gather round lower edge and continue stuffing, then push a small flattened disc of Plasticine inside gathers before pulling up gathers tightly and fastening off. Push in raw edges and oversew to completely close gathers.

Sew beads to head for eyes, taking thread through from one side of head to the other. Cut two pairs of front flippers from sock fabric

and oversew them together in pairs round the edges leaving short straight edges open. Turn right side out and sew upper portion to sides of seal at front as shown in the illustration. Cut four back flipper pieces and make as for front flippers. Sew to back of seal at lower edge.

Crocodile

Cut one pair of crocodile body pieces from sock fabric. Back-stitch them together round edges leaving a gap for turning as shown on the pattern. Turn right side out and stuff, then ladder-stitch gap.

Tie a strand of green thread round neck as shown on pattern, then continue winding thread round and round body at 5mm (¼in) intervals working towards end of tail. Sew end of thread into body. Sew eyes to head as for Seal. Cut two tiny circles of felt for nostrils and stick them in place. Cut four pairs of leg pieces and oversew them together in pairs round the edges, leaving short straight edges open. Turn right side out and sew to crocodile at positions shown on pattern.

THE CHILDREN

You will need: Scraps of brightly coloured felt; card; Plasticine; pink or white stockinette; stretch towelling sock fabric in suitable colours for hair; narrow ribbon; stuffing; black permanent marker pen; red pencil; adhesive.

Note: 5mm (¼in) seams are allowed unless otherwise stated.

To make

Cut the body from coloured felt. (To make slightly taller children you can cut the body strip a little deeper if desired.) Oversew the short edges together and turn right side out. Cut the base circle from card and slip it 5mm (¼in) inside one end of the body. Glue the edge of the felt onto card base. Put a small lump of Plasticine inside the body then press it flat against the base with the end of a pencil. Stuff body then gather round top edge.

Cut the head from stockinette with most stretch in fabric going across the width as shown on the pattern. Join centre back edges of strip. Run a gathering thread round one remaining raw edge, pull up tightly and fasten off. Turn head right side out and stuff, then gather round remaining raw edge, pull up tightly and fasten off. Put the gathered edge of head inside body, noting that both seams will be at back of doll. Pull up body gathers tightly and fasten off, then sew to head gathers.

Now stab-stitch through body from centre front to back for about 2cm (¾in) up from base, pulling stitches tightly to form the legs. Use permanent pen to mark two semi-circles for shoes at base of body.

Mark two black dots for eyes half-way down the face. Take a stitch through from back of head to centre of each eye and back again, pulling thread tightly to indent the eyes. Work mouth with red thread, then colour cheeks and position of nose with pencil.

Cut the hair circle from sock fabric. Turn in and run a gathering thread round the raw edge. Put hair on head and pull up gathers. Sew hair in place stretching sock fabric to fit over the head.

Cut two arm pieces from stockinette with most stretch going across width as shown. Join long edges of each arm and round off at one short end. Trim seam and turn right side out. Push a little stuffing in hand. Cut two sleeve pieces from felt to match body. Wrap a sleeve around each arm and oversew short edges together. Oversew tops of sleeves, catching arm fabric in the stitches.

Sew tops of arms to sides of body varying the angle slightly as shown in the illustration. Tie a 10cm (4in) strip of ribbon round the neck for a scarf, fraying out the ends. Stick ends of scarf to body to hold in place.

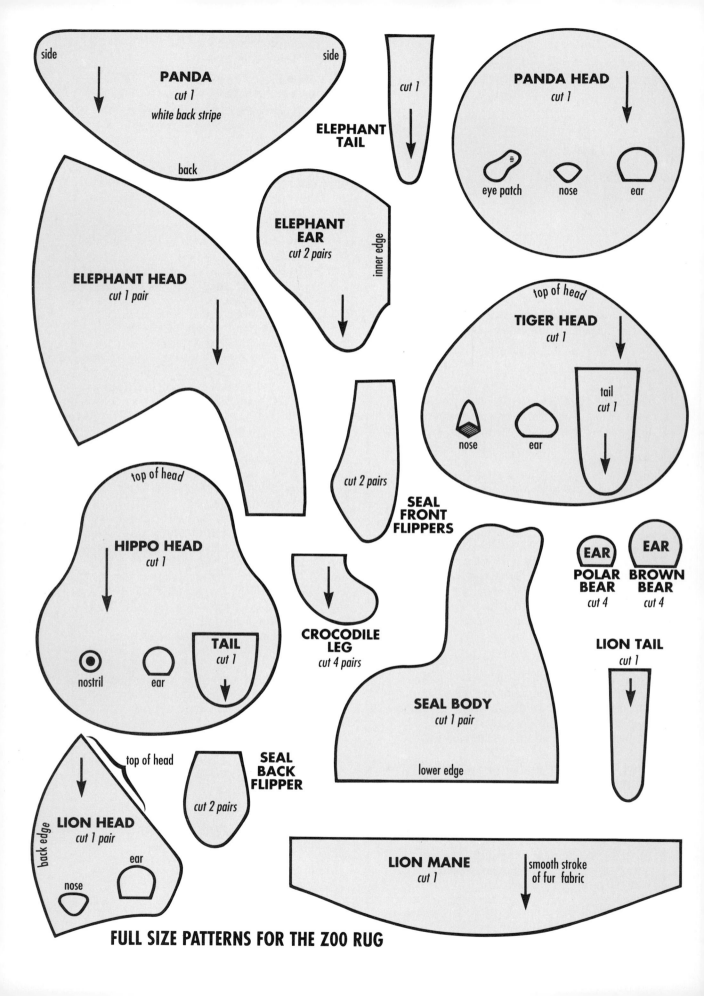

FULL SIZE PATTERNS FOR THE ZOO RUG

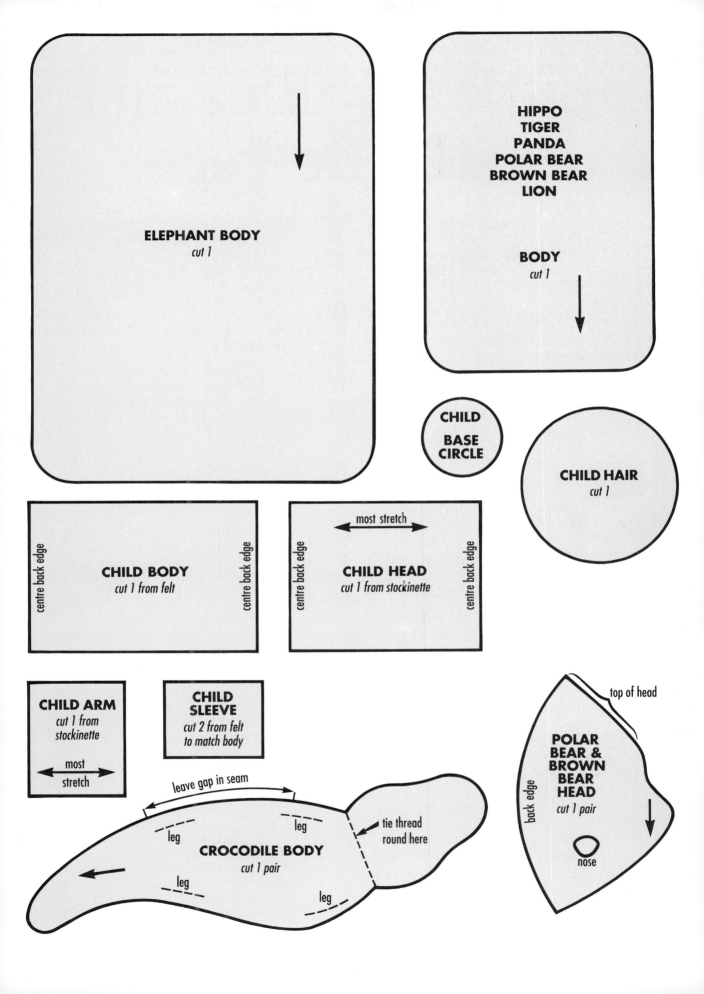

Little Boy Blue and Little Bo-Peep

Each of these nursery characters is about 38cm (15in) tall. The clothing is incorporated into the basic construction, so the dolls are very easy to make from oddments of fabric and cotton stockinette.

For Bo-Peep you will need: 45cm (½yd) of 91cm (36in) wide fabric for dress and hat; 80cm (⅞yd) of ribbon; 1.20m (1¼yd) of ric-rac braid; 90cm (1yd) of gathered lace edging; 225g (½lb) of stuffing.

For Boy Blue you will need: 30cm (⅜yd) of 91cm (36in) wide fabric for smock; 90cm (1yd) of narrow lace edging; 225g (½lb) stuffing; oddment of fabric and knitting yarn for hat; ric-rac braid for trimming the pants.

You will also need: (for both dolls): Oddments of fabric for pants; felt; pink or white cotton stockinette for heads and hands; fur fabric for hair; elastic; strong thread for gathering; adhesive; red pencil for colouring cheeks.

Notes: Trace patterns off the page but trace off shoe pattern, placing folded edge of paper to dotted line shown. Cut out and open up pattern. If making up both dolls, cut paper patterns for the rectangular pieces mentioned in the instructions to save measuring each time. Mark details on patterns. 1cm (⅜in) seams, turnings and hems are allowed throughout.

BO-PEEP

Cut two pants pieces, placing the edge indicated to fold in fabric each time. Work a tacking thread on each piece as shown on the pattern. Join pieces to each other at one centre edge. Clip curve and trim seam.

For the bodice, cut a 9x26cm (3½x10¼in) strip of fabric and join one long edge to the waist edge of pants. For the head, cut a 16cm wide x 18cm long (6¼x7in) strip of stockinette with most stretch going across the 16cm (6¼in) width. Join one short edge to the remaining long edge of bodice, stretching the stockinette to fit.

For centre back seam of doll, join the long edges of head, then short edges of bodice and remaining centre edges of pants. Clip curve in seam as before. Bring centre seams of pants together, then join inside leg edges of each leg. Clip seam. Turn right side out.

Stuff legs, body and lower part of head. Gather ankle edge of each leg, pull up tightly and fasten off. To shape the neck, run a strong doubled thread round neck edge of head, pull up very tightly and knot ends. Sew ends into neck. Finish stuffing the head, then gather up raw edge tightly and fasten off.

Pin the shoe pattern to two layers of felt.

NURSERY-RHYME CONVERSATION

You see in this picture a fat woolly sheep
With Little Boy Blue and Little Bo-Peep.
They've stopped for a chat, it's a beautiful day,
Let's finish the rhyme and find out what
    they say.

'I'm really fed up with those nasty old sheep,'
Says Little Boy Blue to Little Bo-Peep.
'They romp in the meadows, I can't shoo
    them out,
My legs are all wobbly from running about!'

'I've had quite enough of those quadrupeds
    too,'
Says Little Bo-Peep to Little Boy Blue.
'Let's leave them to wander and if you agree,
We'll go and buy muffins and crumpets for tea.'

Stitch round close to edge of pattern. Mark slit line on the felt. Remove the pattern and cut slit in one layer of felt only. Turn right side out through slit and stuff shoe. Pin, then ladder-stitch shoes to gathered ends of pants having the tacked lines on the pants at position of circle shown on the shoe pattern. Sew two lace frills round each ankle and one frill round neck.

For skirt, cut a 14x91cm (5½x36in) strip from same fabric as bodice. Stitch on ric-rac 3cm (1¼in) away from one long edge. Join short edges of strip then hem the edge nearest to ric-rac. Gather remaining long edge round the waist seam on doll, pull up tightly and fasten off. Space out gathers evenly, then sew them to the doll. Tie ribbon round the waist raw edges, ending in a bow at the back. Sew long edges of the ribbon to doll.

Use red thread to work a U-shape in back stitches for mouth 2.5cm (1in) up from the neck. Cut the eyes from black felt. Stick them to face 2cm (¾in) above the mouth and 2.5cm (1in) apart. Colour cheeks and nose with red pencil. For hair cut a 5x30cm (2x12in) strip of fur fabric with smooth stroke going towards one long edge. Oversew the short edges of strip together. Turn right side out. Put hair on the doll's head, with smooth stroke going towards the face, placing this edge 2cm (¾in) above the eyes at front and just above neck at back. Sew the long edges to head.

For the hat, cut a 22x70cm (8¾x27½in) strip of fabric to match dress. Join short edges. Turn in one long edge 5cm (2in) and stitch down the raw edge leaving a gap in stitching for inserting the elastic. Stitch again 1cm (⅜in) away from first stitching line. Thread elastic through to fit head. Gather up remaining long raw edge of hat tightly then fasten off. Cover this gathered raw edge by sewing on a gathered and stuffed 6cm (2½in) diameter circle of fabric. Stuff hat lightly then sew it to the head through gathers, overlapping the top edge of the hair. Sew ribbon bow to front.

For each sleeve, cut a 14x16cm (5½x6¼in) strip of fabric to match dress. Join long edges of each sleeve. Sew across one short end at the seam line with running stitches through both thicknesses of fabric. Pull stitches up tightly and fasten off. Turn sleeve right side out and stuff lightly. Turn in remaining raw edge 2cm (¾in), then run a gathering thread round sleeve, 1.5cm (½in) away from fold.

Cut four hand pieces from stockinette. Join them in pairs leaving wrist edges open. Trim seam, turn right side out and stuff. Gather round each hand, 1cm (⅜in) away from the raw edge, pull up tightly and fasten off. Slip sleeves over hands matching the gathering lines. Pull up sleeve gathers tightly and sew to hands. Sew ric-rac round the gathers. Sew upper portions of sleeves to sides of the doll as illustrated. Bend sleeves at the 'elbows' and catch the folds in place.

Bo-Peep's Crook

You will need: Four pipe cleaners; a plastic drinking straw; a length of sports shoelace; scrap of ribbon.

Join the pipe cleaners to each other in pairs twisting them together for 2cm (¾in) at one end. Twist these pairs together all along the length. Push one end right inside the full length of the straw (the other end of the cleaners will protrude for the bent portion of the crook). Now push the entire crook inside the length of shoelace. Turn in and gather round the raw ends of shoelace. Bend top of crook to shape and tie on a ribbon bow.

BOY BLUE

Make as for Bo-Peep except for the following: Sew ric-rac round lower ends of pants instead of lace trimming. Make skirt portion of his smock as for Bo-Peep's skirt using a 10x42cm (4x16½in) strip of fabric. Sew lace trimming to hem. Turn in the raw waist edge and gather round the fold. Pull up gathers around doll 2cm (¾in) above the waist seam. Sew gathers to doll.

For the cap, gather a 30cm (11¾in) diameter circle of fabric to fit the head as illustrated, then bind this gathered edge with a 6cm (2⅜in) wide fabric strip. Sew a tassel made from yarn to centre top. Stuff cap lightly then sew it to head through the gathers. Pull the top over to one side and catch it down with a stitch or two.

For the collar, cut an 8x26cm (3x10¼in) strip of fabric to match smock. Join long edges and across short ends leaving a gap in seam for turning. Trim seam, turn right side out, then slip-stitch gap. Sew lace to all but the folded edge of collar. Gather the folded edge round doll's neck, pull up tightly, catching ends together at centre front. Sew on ribbon bow.

Boy Blue's Horn

You will need: Scraps of felt; stuffing, a 35cm (14in) length of narrow braid.

Pin the paper pattern to two layers of felt. Cut the felt level with top edge of pattern. Stitch all round, close to other edges of pattern. Remove the pattern and cut out horn close to stitching line. Turn right side out and stuff. Push a 2.5cm (1in) diameter circle of card inside the top edge, then gather this edge up tightly and fasten off. Sew on a circle of felt the same size as card. Sew one end of the braid round top of horn and the other end of braid round horn near to the opposite end as shown in the illustration.

FULL-SIZE PATTERNS FOR LITTLE BOY BLUE AND LITTLE BO BEEP

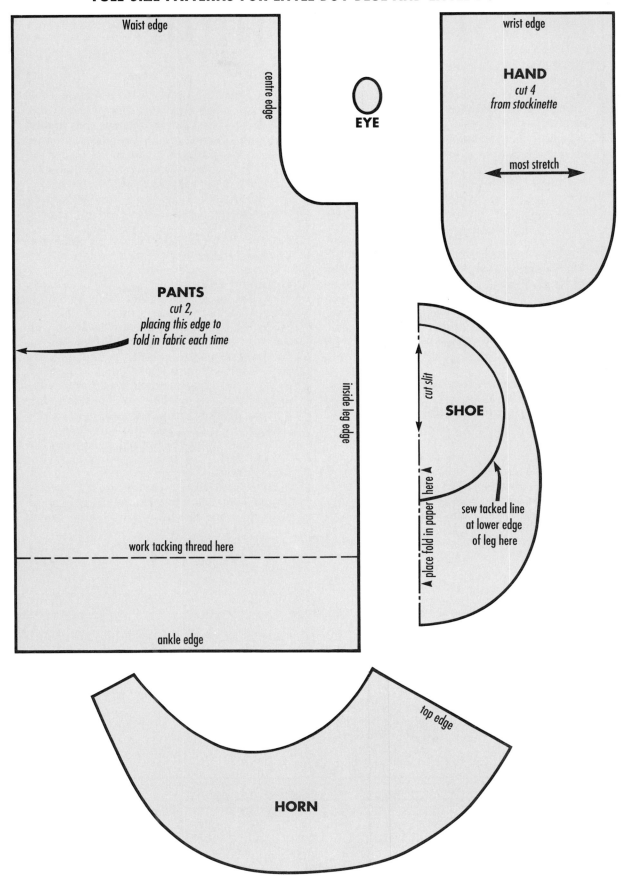

Waist edge

centre edge

PANTS
*cut 2,
placing this edge to
fold in fabric each time*

inside leg edge

work tacking thread here

ankle edge

EYE

wrist edge

HAND
*cut 4
from stockinette*

most stretch

cut slit

SHOE

place fold in paper here

sew tacked line
at lower edge
of leg here

HORN

top edge

Simple Chimps

You can make this floppy chimpanzee as a soft toy, or turn him into an acrobat hanging by his feet or hands from a trapeze. He measures 46cm (18in) from hat to toe and his head is made from a stretch towelling sock.

You will need: A man's brown or fawn stretch towelling sock (to fit shoe size 6–11); small pieces of thin woven cotton fabric for the arms and legs (any colour, as it will not be seen); small pieces of felt – cream for the face, ears and hands: coloured for the shoes, hat and bobbles: black and brown for facial features; 50cm (⅝yd) of 91cm (36in) wide fabric for the suit and the neck frill; 30cm (⅜yd) of 91cm (36in) wide fabric for the contrasting neck, wrist and ankle frills; small piece of ric-rac braid for trimming the hat; small amount of stuffing; adhesive.

For the acrobat you will need: A 6cm (2½in) long strip of furry Velcro hook and loop fastener to match the shoes and the same amount to match the hands.

Notes: 1cm (⅜in) seams and turnings are allowed on all pieces unless otherwise stated.

All patterns are printed full size on the page except for the suit pattern. This is given as a simple rectangular diagram with measure-ments; draw out on paper to the sizes given and mark on all details.

Trace the head pattern off page (the shaded area only). The head pattern is shown on the page in the position it should be placed on the sock, but note that different makes of sock may vary slightly across the width. If the sock *is* wider than the one shown, simply carry on sewing the top head stitching line to the edge of the sock.

Trace all other patterns off the page and mark on all details.

Head and Body
Turn the sock inside out, then pin head pattern to the sock as shown on page 99. Stitch the top head stitching line level with the top edge of the pattern. Now use a coloured pencil to mark the neck line on the sock level with the lower edge of pattern. Remove the pattern and pin it to reverse side of sock to mark on the neck line there also. Remove the pattern and trim off the sock just above the top head stitching line. Now run a very loose contrast-coloured tacking thread around the sock at the marked neck line. Turn head right side out.

Stuff head firmly as far as the tacking thread, taking care to push out the heel of the sock to shape the front of the face. Run a

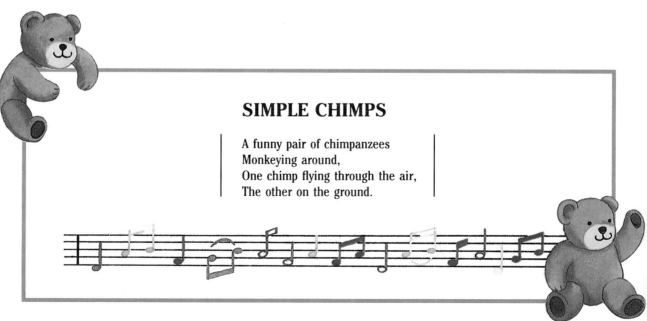

SIMPLE CHIMPS

A funny pair of chimpanzees
Monkeying around,
One chimp flying through the air,
The other on the ground.

strong gathering thread round sock at position of coloured tacking thread. Pull up the gathers very tightly and knot thread ends, then sew ends into the head.

Continue stuffing the remainder of the sock for the body until it measures about 15cm (6in) long from neck to lower edge. Turn in remainder of the sock if necessary and oversew the edges together across the lower edge of the body.

Legs and Shoes

For each leg, cut two 9x18cm (3½x7in) pieces of cotton fabric. Join the pieces at long edges and turn right side out.

Pin the shoe pattern onto two layers of felt. Stitch all round close to the edge of pattern. Now mark the small dots shown on pattern onto the felt, by pushing a pencil point through dots. Remove the pattern and cut out the shoe close to the stitching line. Pull apart the two layers of felt and cut a slit in one piece only from one dot to the other as shown on the pattern. Turn shoe right side out through slit and stuff firmly.

Now turn in one end of the leg and pin it to the shoe at the oval dotted line to cover the slit with leg seams facing centre front and back. Slip-stitch the leg edge to shoe as pinned. Stuff the leg lightly but evenly. Turn in top raw edge of leg then bring the seams together and oversew, pulling the stitches tightly to gather. Sew the legs to lower edge of the body. Now sew a 3cm (1¼in) strip of furry Velcro to the top of each shoe (if making acrobat).

Ankle Frills

For each ankle frill, cut a 7x36cm (2¾x14in) strip of contrast fabric. Join short edges of each strip. Now fold each strip in half, with right side outside and bringing long raw edges together. Run a gathering thread round, 1cm (⅜in) from raw edges. Slip a frill over each shoe and pull up gathering thread round the ankle. Fasten off thread, then space out gathers evenly. Sew frill to leg through the gathering line.

Suit

Cut two pairs of suit pieces. Join the pairs at centre edges then clip curves in seams. Join the pairs to each other at side edges, then the inside leg edges. Turn suit right side out and put it on the chimpanzee. Turn in the neck edge and run round a strong gathering thread. Pull up gathers tightly around the neck and fasten off. Adjust the gathers so that suit side

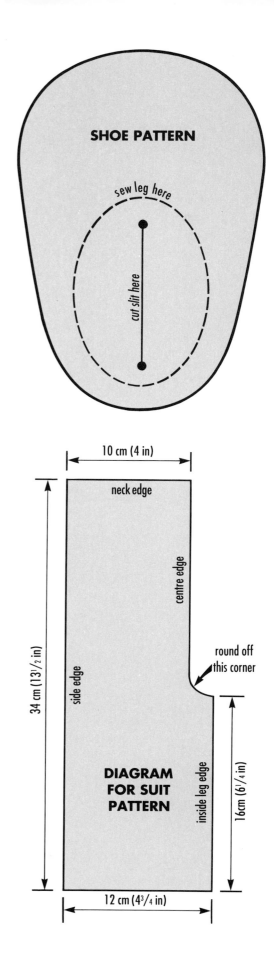

SHOE PATTERN

sew leg here

cut slit here

10 cm (4 in)

neck edge

centre edge

round off this corner

34 cm (13½ in)

side edge

inside leg edge

16cm (6¼ in)

DIAGRAM FOR SUIT PATTERN

12 cm (4¾ in)

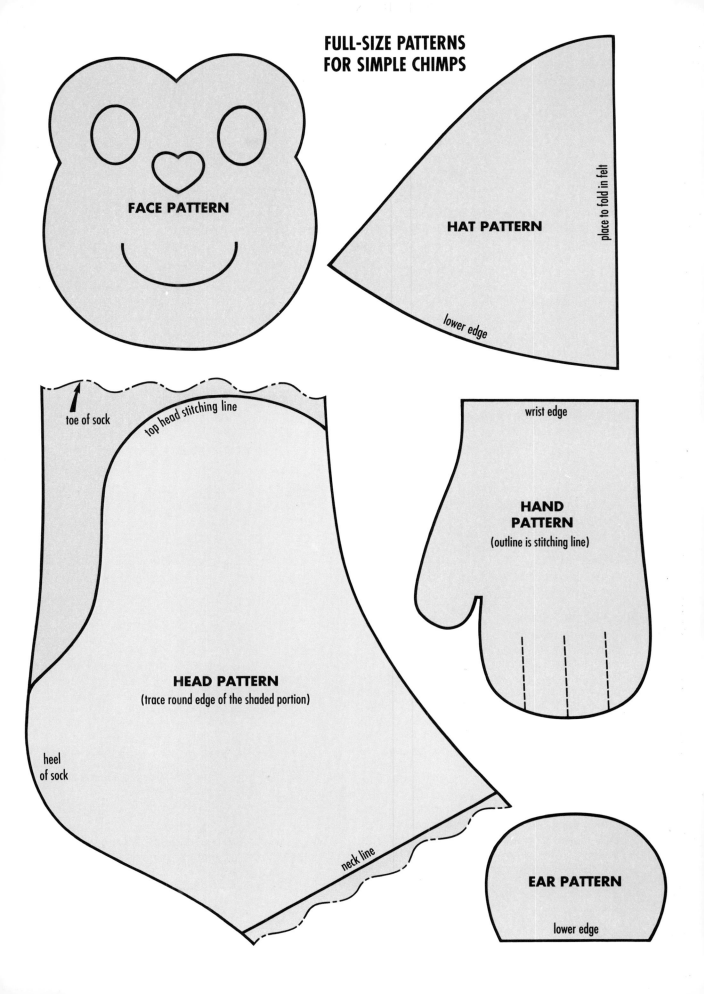

FULL-SIZE PATTERNS
FOR SIMPLE CHIMPS

FACE PATTERN

HAT PATTERN

place to fold in felt

lower edge

toe of sock

top head stitching line

wrist edge

HAND
PATTERN
(outline is stitching line)

HEAD PATTERN
(trace round edge of the shaded portion)

heel
of sock

neck line

EAR PATTERN

lower edge

seams are at sides and centre seams are at centre front and back.

Now let the head fall forward onto the chest. Sew securely in this position where the head touches chest under the chin, taking stitches through the suit and into the body.

Run a gathering thread round each ankle edge of the suit 1cm (⅜in) from raw edge, turn in raw edge and pull up gathers round the ankle frill gathers, then fasten off. Space out gathers evenly then sew to frill gathers.

Cut three 5cm (2in) diameter circles of felt for bobbles down front of the suit. Gather round edge of each circle and stuff the centre, pulling gathers up tightly. Fasten off thread and sew bobbles in place.

Neck Frills

For the contrast neck frill, cut a 14x70cm (5½x28in) strip of fabric. For a frill which matches the suit, cut a 12x60cm (4¾x24in) strip, joining pieces to make up the full length if necessary. Make neck frills as for the ankle frills. Gather round the raw edges of each frill, slip over head, then pull up gathers tightly round neck and fasten off thread.

Arms, Hands and Wrist Frills

For each arm, cut two 8x17cm (3x6¾in) pieces of cotton fabric. Join the pieces at long edges and turn right side out.

Pin the hand pattern to two layers of cream felt, then cut felt level with wrist edge of pattern. Stitch all round, close to other edges of pattern, leaving wrist edges open. Remove pattern and cut out hand close to the stitching line. Turn hand right side out and stuff lightly. Machine-stitch through hands at positions of dotted lines, to divide into fingers. Pull the thread ends through and knot them, then sew into hands.

Turn in one raw edge of each arm and slip it 1cm (⅜in) over wrist edge of hand, with arm seams level with hand seams. Slip-stitch arm to hand, easing in the arm fabric to fit hand. Stuff the arms lightly but evenly. Turn in top raw edge of each arm and oversew, pulling stitches to gather up tightly. Pin an arm to each side of the body about 3cm (1¼in) down from the neck having thumbs pointing towards the front. Sew arms in place taking stitches through the suit and into the body. Now sew a 3cm (1¼in) strip of furry Velcro to the palm of each hand (if making acrobat). Make and sew on the wrist frills as for the ankle frills.

Sleeves

For each sleeve, cut an 18x20cm (7x8in) piece of the suit fabric. Join the short edges of each piece. Turn right side out, then slip a sleeve over each arm with sleeve seams underneath the arms. Gather, turn in, and sew wrist edges to the wrist frills in same way as for the ankle edges of suit. Run a gathering thread round the top of each sleeve 1cm (⅜in) away from raw edge. Turn in raw edges, then pull up gathers tightly round tops of arms and fasten off. Sew gathered edges of sleeves to the suit.

Face and Ears

Cut the face piece from cream felt and mark on the mouth. Stretch the face piece at the centre of the mouth area, pushing the felt out to a rounded shape so that it will fit over the rounded towelling face. Now using black thread, machine-stitch along the mouth line a few times, or alternatively back-stitch by hand. Slip-stitch the face piece in place as shown in the illustration. Cut the nose from brown felt and glue it in place. Cut the eyes from black felt and work a small highlight on each one using white thread. Glue the eyes in place.

Pin the ear pattern onto two layers of cream felt, then cut out felt level with lower edge of the pattern. Stitch, cut out and turn ears as for the hands. Now oversew lower edges of each ear together pulling stitches to gather. Sew the ears to each side of head as shown in the illustration.

Hat

Cut two hat pieces from felt placing edge of pattern indicated to fold in felt each time. Join the pieces taking a 3mm (⅛in) seam and leaving lower edges open. Turn the hat right side out and push a little stuffing in the top. Place the hat on head as illustrated and pin the lower edge in place. Slip-stitch lower edge to head, pushing in more stuffing a little at a time to make a firm rounded shape. Sew ric-rac round the lower edge of hat and add a felt bobble to the top, made as for the suit bobbles.

Trapeze

Use a piece of thick wooden dowelling about 40cm (16in) in length. Glue a strip of hooked Velcro round and round the dowelling, so that chimp's hands and feet may be attached. Use thick cord or rope to suspend the trapeze. Glue a large bead to each end.

Four Bears

Four miniature teddies – all very easy to make from stretch towelling socks and oddments of fabric. There is a garland decoration for the door, a Christmas tree fairy, a clown to decorate the nursery and a little bean-bag teddy toy in a stocking. Each teddy measures 13cm (5in), excluding hats.

For the teddies you will need: Men's pale yellow or white stretch towelling socks; oddments of printed and plain fabrics, ribbon and stuffing; a little black double-knitting yarn; iron-on medium superstretch Vilene interfacing; thin card; adhesive.

In addition you will need: For the teddy in a stocking: plastic beans or lentils, oddment of broderie anglaise trimming; **For the garland:** corrugated reinforced card cut from grocery boxes, 30cm (⅜yd) of 91cm (36in) wide red printed fabric, a little cotton wool, 1.30m (1½yd) of white guipure flower trimming, oddments of dark blue felt and wide ribbon, a 2.5cm (1in) strip of Velcro hook and loop fastener, two tiny buttons for teddy; **For the fairy:** oddments of shiny blue fabric, net fabric and wide and narrow silver braid, 50cm (20in) length of 2cm (¾in) wide silver braid, 80cm (⅞yd) each of miniature blue and silver tinsel, for the wand – a cocktail stick, a piece of kitchen foil and fuse wire, two silver or white guipure flowers and narrow ribbon, a small elastic band or wire for securing the teddy to tree top; **For the nursery (clown) teddy:** cuttings off a red stretch towelling sock or similar fabric, 1m (1⅛yd) of thin cord, narrow ric-rac, 35cm (14in) length of 2.5cm (1in) wide soft ribbon for neck frill, two guipure flowers.

Patterns: The patterns are printed full size for tracing off the page. Trace the body pattern onto thin folded paper, placing fold in paper to edge indicated. Cut out and open up the pattern, then glue it onto thin card. Cut out the card level with the pattern. Trace off all other patterns and cut out, then mark on details.

Notes: Seams are as stated in the instructions. When buying socks to make the teddies note that acrylic/nylon mixture socks give best results. These socks are also about half the price of 100% cotton ones. You should be able to make about six teddy heads from one sock. When gathering, use double thread for strength.

Safety note: If making the clown teddy as a decoration for a baby's room, take care to keep it out of the baby's reach, so that the cord could not be a danger.

FOUR BEARS

A Teddy in a snowstorm,
A Teddy for the tree,
A Teddy for the nursery,
And one for ME!

To prepare the sock material

Cut open the sock at centre back from the top edge and right around the toe. Trim off and discard the elasticated band at the top of the sock. Open up the sock and lay it flat with the wrong side uppermost. Cut a piece of interfacing to fit the straight *leg portion* of the sock, noting that the widthways stretch of the interfacing should go across the *width* of sock fabric. Use a steam iron, or damp cloth and ordinary iron, to bond the interfacing to the sock. Repeat this with the foot portion of the sock.

The loops in the sock fabric usually run smoothly from the toe end to the elasticated top. Take care to cut out the pieces with the smooth stroke of the loops in direction shown on the pattern pieces.

To make the teddy head

Each teddy is the same. Cut one head piece, pinning the pattern to the interfacing side of sock fabric. Before removing the pattern, push a pencil point through eye dot on pattern to mark fabric. Reverse pattern and cut and mark second head piece in the same way. Now push the pencil point right through the fabric head pieces to mark the dots on right side. Join the head pieces by oversewing them together round the edges, leaving lower edges open. Machine-stitch just within the oversewing. Turn right side out. Run a gathering thread round the neck at the position shown on the pattern.

Stuff the head *very* firmly until it is completely rounded as shown in the illustration. Take care to stuff the snout also, pushing in stuffing with scissor points. Put your index finger inside the neck, pull up gathers tightly around your finger and fasten off. Stuff the neck to fill it.

For one eye, cut a 30cm (12in) length of black yarn. Tie a knot at the centre winding yarn around three times before pulling knot tight. Thread a darning needle with one end of the yarn. Insert needle at one eye dot and pass it through the head to come out at the neck stuffing. Take the other end of yarn through the head in the same way, inserting the needle just above the dot. Pull yarn ends tightly and knot them together, then trim off excess length. Repeat for the other eye.

Make a knot for the nose in the same way, but wind the yarn around four times instead of three before pulling it tight. Sew the nose knot into end of snout in the same way as for the eyes, but keep the knot horizontal.

Cut four ear pieces from sock fabric.

Oversew them together in pairs, leaving the lower edges open. Turn right side out. Oversew lower edges of each ear together, pulling stitches tightly to gather slightly. Sew the ears to sides of head, placing them 2.5cm (1in) apart at top of the head.

BEAN-BAG TEDDY IN A STOCKING

Make the head as described above.

Body

Cut a 13x30cm (5x12in) piece of printed fabric and iron a piece of interfacing onto the wrong side. Fold the piece in half with the right side inside and pin the short edges together. Draw round the card body pattern with a pencil, onto interfacing. Pin the layers together inside the drawn shape. Trim fabric level with the neck edge line. Stitch all round the drawn line. Cut out the body 3mm (⅛in) away from stitching line. Turn right side out.

Stuff the arms and legs lightly. Turn in the neck edge at dotted line shown on pattern and run a gathering thread round the folded edge. Fill the body with beans. Now push the open lower edge of head right inside the body. Pull up the body gathers tightly around the neck gathers on head, then fasten off. Sew body gathers to neck gathers. Tie a ribbon bow round the teddy's neck.

Stocking

Cut a 15x24cm (6x9½in) piece of printed fabric and iron interfacing to the wrong side. Cut out one pair of stocking pieces. Join the centre front edges for about 5cm (2in) only, taking a 3mm (⅛in) seam. Open out the pieces and fold down the top edge to wrong side, at dotted line shown on the pattern. Catch this raw edge in place. On the right side of fabric, stitch the trimming to folded top edge with edges of trimming and stocking level. Now join the remainder of stocking seam. Turn right side out and press.

CHRISTMAS GARLAND

For the garland draw a 22cm (8¾in) diameter circle on a piece of card and using the same centre point draw a 34cm (13½in) diameter circle also. Cut out the card at both lines to form the garland ring. Cut once through the width of the ring so that the tube of fabric can be threaded onto the card.

Cut two 15cm (6in) wide strips across full width of printed fabric. Join them to each other at one short edge taking a narrow seam. Join long edges of strip taking a 5mm (¼in) seam. Tack across one short end, then push

this end through with a ruler to turn the fabric tube right side out. Remove the tacking thread.

Now thread the strip onto the garland ring, having the seam in fabric at centre back of the card. When all the fabric is threaded on, rejoin the cut ends of the card ring with sticky tape. Lap one selvedge end of the fabric over

the other and slip-stitch in place. Space out the gathers in fabric evenly all round the ring. Sew a loop of ribbon to back of ring having the top of the loop level with the outer edge of the fabric. Take a stitch or two through the ribbon loop and card to secure the loop.

For the background piece, cut a 31cm (12¼in) diameter circle of card. Glue it to a piece of dark blue felt, then cut out the felt about 2cm (¾in) larger all round than the card circle. Turn and glue this extra to the other side of the card. To neaten this side of the card circle, glue on a slightly smaller circle of thin card or paper.

Mark a line across the blue felt as shown in Diagram 1. Glue a layer of cotton wool level with and below this line for snow, as shown in Diagram 1. Now spread glue liberally round the outer edge of the blue felt background circle on the right side. Press it centrally in position at the back of the garland ring, having the snow at right angles to and directly opposite the hanging loop.

Glue a length of guipure flower trim all round the garland on right side near to edge. Decorate the top of the garland with ribbon bows and a rosette as illustrated.

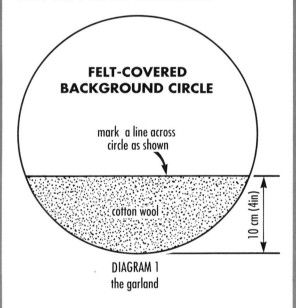

DIAGRAM 1
the garland

Teddy

Make as for Bean-bag Teddy, but stuff the body instead of filling it with beans. Sew the two buttons to front of body. Tie a length of ribbon round the neck for a scarf. Sew the furry Velcro strip to the back of the body.

Place teddy on the background circle in the position illustrated. Mark the position of teddy's Velcro strip on the blue felt where it touches. Glue the hooked strip of Velcro to the blue felt at this position. Note that the glue must be applied liberally in order to soak through the felt to the card backing. Press the Velcro strip firmly in place from time to time as the glue dries. When the glue is dry, press teddy in position. Now cut single guipure flowers off the trimming and glue them around teddy for snowflakes.

FAIRY TEDDY

Make the head as described on page 102.

Body

Trace the body pattern off the page as for other teddies but trim off the arms at dotted line shown. Glue the remaining pattern piece to card and make the body from blue shiny fabric in the same way as for the bean bag, filling with stuffing instead of beans. Attach the body to head in the same way also.

Arms

Cut four arm pieces from sock fabric using the pattern given. Oversew them together in pairs, leaving the inner edges open. Machine-stitch just within the oversewing. Turn the arms right side out. Stuff them lightly, then oversew the inner edges of each arm together. Sew the arms to side seams of body, just below the neck.

Skirt

Cut a 14x50cm (5½x20in) strip of shiny blue fabric. Join the short edges, taking a narrow seam. Press the seam open. Narrowly hem one long edge. Glue on 2cm (¾in) wide silver braid level with this edge. Gather round the remaining raw edge, pull up the gathers tightly around teddy just beneath arms, then fasten off. Space out the gathers evenly, having the skirt seam at centre back. Sew the gathers to body.

Glue a strip of narrow silver braid round the gathers to cover raw edge. Glue same narrow braid over shoulders to form a V-point at centre front as illustrated. Glue a small ribbon bow to the neck of dress at front.

Crown head-dress

Form a 10cm (5½in) length of wide braid into a circle by lapping and glueing the ends. Glue to top of the head between ears.

Wings

Cut a 14x22cm (5½x8¾in) strip of net fabric and round off all the corners. Sew or glue miniature blue and silver tinsel round the edges. Gather up the strip tightly at centre and sew gathers to back of teddy below the neck.

Wand

Cover the cocktail stick by winding and glueing a narrow strip of kitchen foil around it. Glue the guipure flowers to one end, sandwiching the stick between them. For the 'halo' around the flowers, wind fuse wire

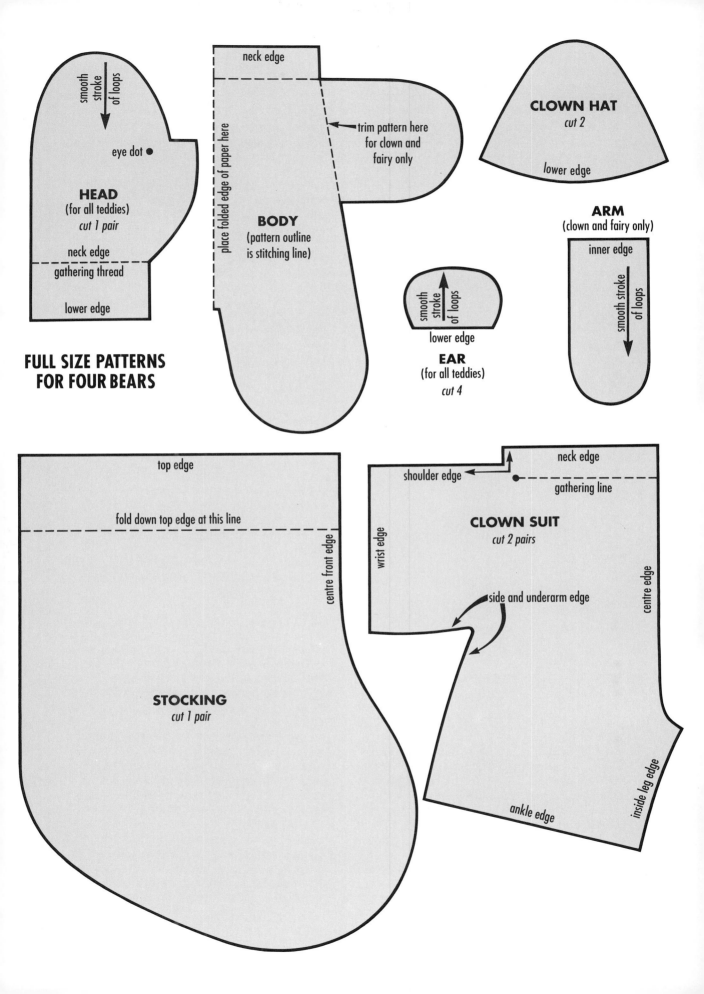

round a little of the miniature silver tinsel. Form it into a circle and secure the wire to cocktail stick below the flowers. Tie a ribbon bow round the wand as illustrated.

Use a bodkin to open up a hole in the teddy's hand, then glue the wand into the hand. Fix the teddy to top of Christmas tree with an elastic band or wire, around the body underneath skirt.

CLOWN TEDDY

Make the head and body in same way as for Fairy, noting that the fabric which you use for the body will only be visible as feet or 'shoes' on the finished teddy.

Arms

Cut the length of cord in half and make a knot in one end of each length. Using sock fabric to match the head, make the arms as for Fairy, but enclose the knotted ends of cord as shown in Diagram 2 when joining the arm pieces. Turn the arms right side out and stuff lightly. Sew the open ends of arms to sides of body just below the neck, taking care to have cords coming out of the 'hands' at top.

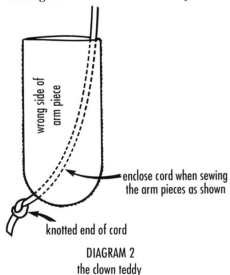

wrong side of arm piece

enclose cord when sewing the arm pieces as shown

knotted end of cord

DIAGRAM 2
the clown teddy

Suit

Take 3mm (⅛in) seams when stitching the suit. Cut two pairs of clown suit pieces and join the pairs at the centre edges. Clip seams at curves, then press them open. Join the pieces at shoulder edges, side and underarm edges and also the inside leg edges. Clip seams at corners and curves, then turn the suit right side out.

Turn in the neck edge at dotted line shown and run a gathering thread round the fold. Put the suit on teddy pushing the legs through neck edge and pulling the arms through the sleeves. Pull up suit gathers tightly around teddy's neck and fasten off. Space out the gathers evenly, then sew them to neck.

Turn in the ankle and wrist edges 5mm (¼in) and run gathering threads round the folded edges. Pull up gathers to fit the legs and arms, then fasten off. Sew the gathers in place, then sew ric-rac round the gathered wrist and ankle edges.

Neck frill

Fold one long edge of the ribbon down 1cm (⅜in) and press. Join the short ends of ribbon. Run a gathering thread round the folded edge, pull up tightly round teddy's neck and fasten off. Space out gathers evenly, and sew them to neck. Sew the two guipure flowers to centre front of suit.

Hat

Using a piece of the same fabric as used for the body (with interfacing bonded on), cut out two hat pieces. Oversew them together leaving lower edges open. Machine-stitch just within the oversewing. Leaving the hat wrong side out, turn up the lower edge 5mm (¼in) and catch it in place. Turn hat right side out and sew ric-rac round and near to the lower edge. Stuff the hat and sew to top of head with the seam in line with teddy's head seam.

Balls

Bond a piece of interfacing to wrong side of the sock or stretch towelling fabric having the widthways stretch of interfacing and fabric in the same direction.

For each ball, cut a 4x6cm (1½x2¼in) strip of fabric, having the length of the strip going across the width of fabric. Join the short edges of strip taking a 3mm (⅛in) seam. Gather round one remaining raw edge. Pull up tightly, then fasten off, taking care not to sew across the centre of the gathers because the cord has to be threaded through. Turn ball right side out.

Run a gathering thread round the remaining raw edge. Stuff the ball firmly, then pull up the gathers tightly, turning in the raw edge. Fasten off as before. Make four balls.

Make a double knot in each cord, 6cm (2¼in) away from each of the teddy's hands. Use a bodkin to thread one ball onto each cord. Knot the cords again 9cm (3½in) above the first knots and thread another ball onto each cord. Knot the ends of the cords together. Make another ball and enclose this knot when gathering up and fastening off the second edge.

Four furry toys

These toys are all made from the same basic body and head shapes, with very slight variations to the outlines. Each animal measures about 38cm (15in) in length.

For each animal you will need: 45cm (½yd) of 138cm (54in) wide fur fabric in the colours and types mentioned in the individual instructions; 450g (1lb) of stuffing; a pair of 13mm (½in) diameter safety eyes (brown for puppy, lamb and lion; blue for the kitten); oddments of black felt and black double-knitting yarn; adhesive.

In addition you will need: For puppy's collar – felt, small buckle and identity tag; for lamb and kitten – an 80cm (⅞yd) length of ribbon; for lion – small pieces of long pile fawn fur fabric (for the mane and tail tip).

Important Note: The body pattern is too large to print on one page. Therefore it is divided into two sections. After tracing off the various patterns (as directed in the following paragraph), join the two body sections with sticky tape at the dotted lines X–Y.

To make the body patterns (same for all animals)

Upper-body pattern: Fold two pieces of thin paper of appropriate size in half, creasing them well at the fold. Open up the folded papers and place creased edge to the edge indicated on each piece of the body pattern.

Trace off the patterns all round the solid black outline and also trace off the semi-circular shaped neck edge. Mark on centre back point and also points A, B and C. Fold the patterns in half again and hold them together with dabs of adhesive placed *outside* the traced outlines. Now cut out the patterns and also cut out the semi-circular neck edge. While patterns are still folded, mark all the points A, B and C on the other halves. Open up the patterns to give the whole upper body pattern. Join them at dotted lines X–Y. You will now have two sets of opposite points A–B on the neck edge. You can use either set of these points when sewing on the head. With one set the head will turn to the left, with the other it will turn to the right.

TOYS IN THE BED

I take my toys to bed each night
And though I'm very wee,
When every one is tucked in tight
There's no room left for me!

Underbody pattern: Fold another two pieces of paper etc as for the upper-body pattern. Trace off pattern outline as before but follow the *dotted line* at back of body between points C. Trace off the underbody dart cutting line also. Fold the patterns again and cut out etc as for the upper body. Cut along the dart cutting line also. Mark on the centre back point and points C. Open up the patterns to give the whole underbody pattern. Join them at dotted lines X–Y.

All other patterns: See individual instructions for each animal.

Notes: Take care when cutting out to have smooth stroke of fur pile in direction indicated by arrows on patterns. After cutting out and before removing patterns, mark on all the points indicated with a pencil. 5mm (¼in) seams are allowed on all pieces except where oversewing of seams is mentioned in instructions.

If you wish to use felt for the eyes instead of safety eyes, cut 13mm (½in) diameter circles from two layers of black felt glued together. Oversew round the edges. Use white thread to work a small highlight on each one, then sew in place at the marked positions.

THE PUPPY

Use brown polished fur fabric.

Trace off the head pattern, following the black outline and mark on position of the eye. Cut out one pair of head pieces and mark the eye position on each one.

* Join head pieces leaving the neck edges open. Pierce a small hole through fur fabric at each marked eye position. Push shank of each eye through from right side to wrong side. Press the washer down firmly onto each shank, having curved points of washer uppermost. Turn the head right side out.

Cut out the upper body, then cut out the neck circle before removing the pattern. Run a gathering thread between points C at back of the upper body. Cut out the underbody piece, then cut the fur fabric level with dart cutting lines before removing the pattern.

Now, having wrong side of upper body uppermost, push the head inside the cut-out neck circle and bring raw edges of circle and neck edge of head together. Match and pin the points A and B on the head to either of the sets of points A and B on the neck circle. Tack the raw edges together, gently stretching the raw edge of neck circle to fit the neck edge of

head. Stitch the seam as tacked, then turn head wrong side out again.

On the underbody piece, stitch the raw edges of the dart together, leaving a 13cm (5in) gap at centre. Now join upper and underbody pieces all round the edges, pulling up gathers in upper body to fit underbody between points C and matching centre back points. Clip seam at inner corners between back legs and body.

Turn right side out and stuff firmly, then ladder-stitch the gap in underbody dart. Trim fur pile just above the eyes. **

Tail
Trace off tail pattern following the dotted line indicated for the puppy. Cut one pair of tail pieces. Oversew pieces together round edges leaving lower edges open. Turn right side out and stuff. Sew open edge of tail to underbody at centre back with tail pointing upwards.

Ears
Trace off puppy's ear pattern by the outline. Cut two pairs of ear pieces and oversew them together in pairs leaving lower edges open. Turn right side out and oversew lower edges of each ear together. Pin, then sew lower edges of ears vertically to sides of head having points E 5cm (2in) apart at top of head. Fold ears forward as illustrated, then catch underside of each one to head, to hold in place.

Nose
Trace off nose pattern for puppy. Glue two layers of black felt together, then cut out nose and oversew all round the edges. Sew nose in place as illustrated.

Collar
Cut a 45cm (18in) long strip from two layers of felt glued together, making width of the strip to suit your buckle. Taper one end to a point then stitch all round the edges of the strip. Attach blunt end to the buckle and make small holes at intervals from the tapered end. Thread on the identity tag and fasten the collar round puppy's neck.

THE LAMB

Use cream curled fur fabric.

Trace off the head pattern by the outline but also follow the dotted lines indicated for lamb. Mark on position of eye. Cut out one pair of head pieces and mark the eye position on each one.

Now make exactly as for Puppy from * to **.

Feet
Trace off lamb's foot pattern. Cut out eight foot pieces from black felt. Oversew the pieces together in pairs leaving upper edges open. Turn down the seam allowance on upper edges and tack. Turn feet right side out. Stretch each foot piece slightly to round out the oversewn edges. Push a foot piece onto the end of each leg and pin, then slip-stitch the upper edges in place.

Tail
Trace off the tail pattern by the outline, then cut one pair of tail pieces. Make as for Puppy's tail. Sew open end of tail to underbody at centre back, with tail curling around the body as illustrated.

Ears
Trace off the ear pattern by the outline but follow the dotted line at lower edge, for Lamb.

Cut and sew the ears as for Puppy. Turn right side out and oversew the lower edges of each ear together, pulling stitches to gather slightly. Pin lower edges of ears to sides of head, with points D about 7cm (2¾in) apart at top of head. Sew lower edges of ears in place.

Nose and mouth

Trace off Lamb's nose pattern, then cut out and sew as for Puppy's nose. Pin the nose in place as illustrated. Using double black yarn work a long horizontal stitch below nose for mouth, knotting ends of yarn beneath nose. Work another stitch over first stitch, then fasten off yarn under nose. Sew nose in place. Trim fur pile above and below mouth and around nose. Tie ribbon in a bow round neck.

THE LION

Use yellow fur fabric for the lion and fawn long pile for the mane and end of tail only.

Trace off the head pattern following the black outline and mark on position of eye. Trace off the cutting line for face edge of lion, then cut your pattern along this line. Mark the pattern pieces 'face piece' and 'mane piece' as shown on pattern.

Cut out one pair of face pieces from yellow fur fabric and mark eye position on each one. Cut one pair of mane pieces from fawn long pile fur fabric. Join the face pieces to mane pieces by oversewing them together at the face edges. Now make exactly as given for Puppy from * to **.

Tail

Trace off, make tail and sew in place in same way as for Lamb. Trace off tail end piece pattern and cut two pieces from long pile fur fabric. Oversew them together round edges leaving upper edges open. Turn down the seam allowance on upper edges and tack. Turn right side out and push in a little stuffing. Slip open end over end of tail and sew in place.

Ears

Trace off the ear pattern and cut out four pieces. Oversew them together in pairs leaving lower edges open. Turn right side out and oversew lower edges together pulling stitches to gather slightly. Brush a little of the mane fur fabric pile forward over face. Sew ears to mane just behind face seam line placing them 5cm (2in) apart at top of head. Trim mane pile above the eyes if necessary.

Nose and mouth

Trace off Lion's nose pattern, then cut and sew as for Puppy's nose. Pin the nose in place as illustrated. Work the mouth in double black yarn starting and fastening off yarn beneath nose. Work a short stitch straight down from nose in double black yarn, then a shallow W at base of this stitch as illustrated. Sew nose in place. Trim fur pile around mouth and above nose.

THE KITTEN

Use grey polished fur fabric

Trace off the head pattern by the outline but also follow the dotted lines indicated for the kitten. Mark on position of the eye. Cut out one pair of head pieces and mark eye position on each one. Now make exactly as for Puppy from * to **.

Tail

Make and sew in place exactly as for Lamb's tail.

Ears

Trace off the ear pattern and cut and make as for Puppy. Turn right side out and oversew lower edges of each ear together, pulling stitches to gather very slightly. Pin the ears to sides of head, having points F about 4cm (1½in) apart at top of head. Sew lower edges of ears in place.

Nose and mouth

Trace off kitten's nose pattern, then cut and sew as for Puppy's nose. Pin nose in place as illustrated. Work the mouth in double black yarn starting and fastening off yarn beneath nose. Using double black yarn, work a short straight stitch down from nose then a small shallow W at base of this stitch as illustrated. Sew nose in place. Trim fur pile around mouth and chin and above nose. Tie ribbon in a bow round neck.

join this edge of body pattern to the other dotted edge, to form the complete pattern

X

Y

smooth stroke of fur pile

A

trace off then cut out this shape for
neck edge on UPPER-BODY pattern only

**FULL-SIZE PATTERNS
FOR FOUR FURRY TOYS**

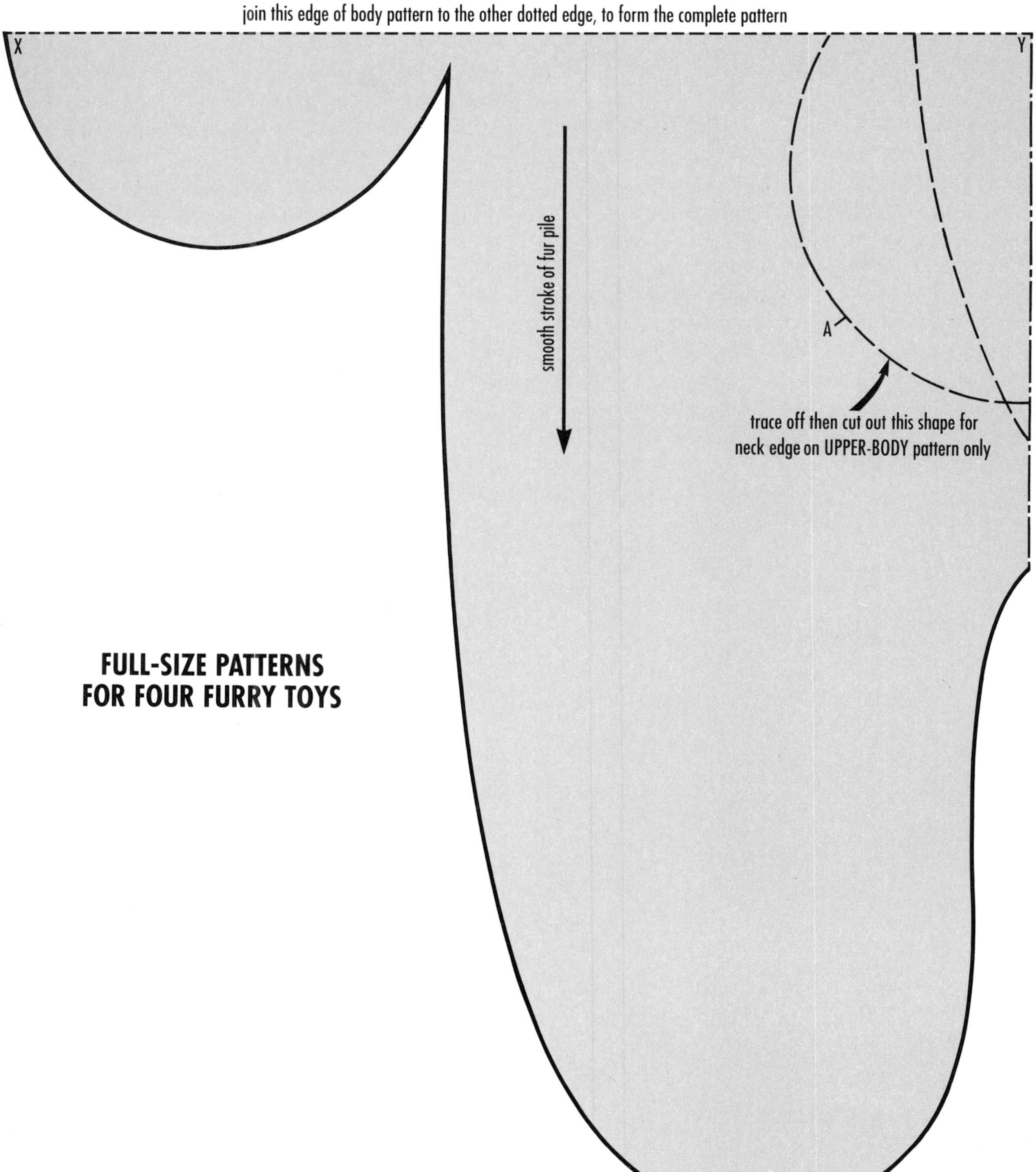

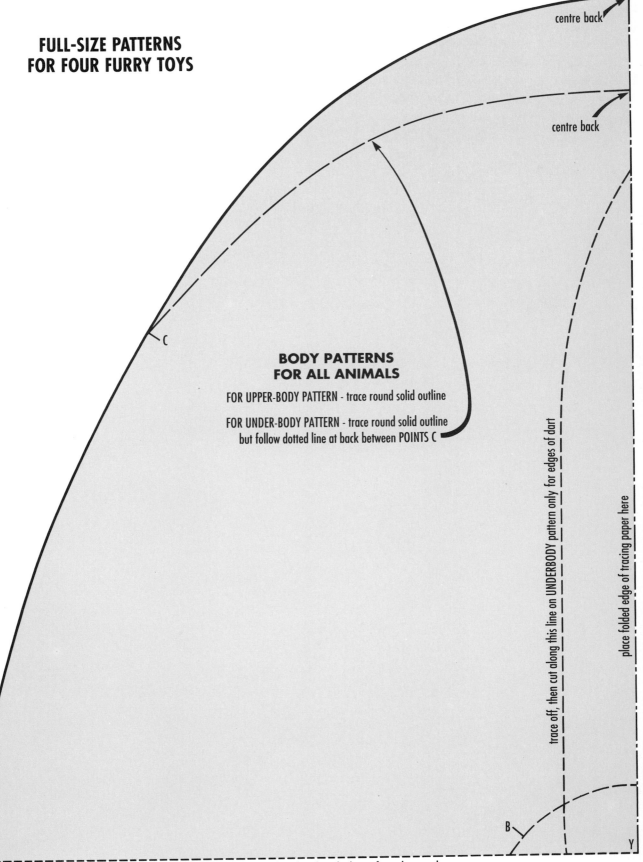

FULL-SIZE PATTERNS FOR FOUR FURRY TOYS

centre back

centre back

C

BODY PATTERNS FOR ALL ANIMALS

FOR UPPER-BODY PATTERN - trace round solid outline

FOR UNDER-BODY PATTERN - trace round solid outline but follow dotted line at back between POINTS C

trace off, then cut along this line on UNDERBODY pattern only for edges of dart

place folded edge of tracing paper here

B

X

Y

Join this edge of body pattern to the other dotted edge to form the complete pattern

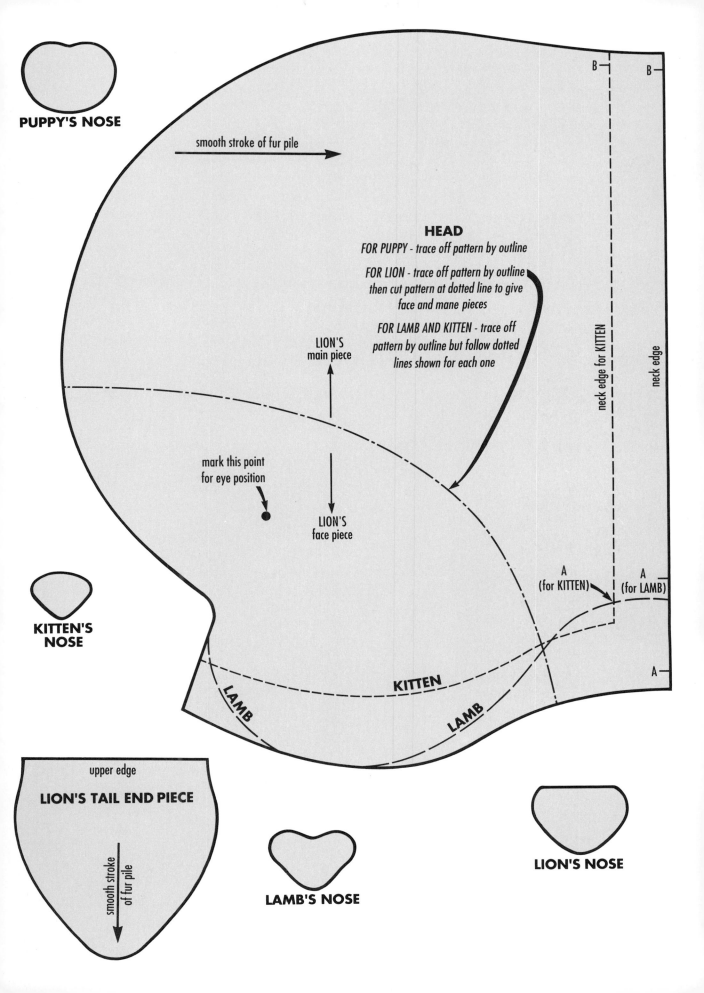

PUPPY'S NOSE

smooth stroke of fur pile

HEAD

FOR PUPPY - trace off pattern by outline

FOR LION - trace off pattern by outline then cut pattern at dotted line to give face and mane pieces

FOR LAMB AND KITTEN - trace off pattern by outline but follow dotted lines shown for each one

B — B

neck edge for KITTEN

neck edge

LION'S main piece

mark this point for eye position

LION'S face piece

A (for KITTEN)

A (for LAMB)

KITTEN'S NOSE

KITTEN

LAMB

LAMB

LAMB

A

upper edge

LION'S TAIL END PIECE

smooth stroke of fur pile

LAMB'S NOSE

LION'S NOSE

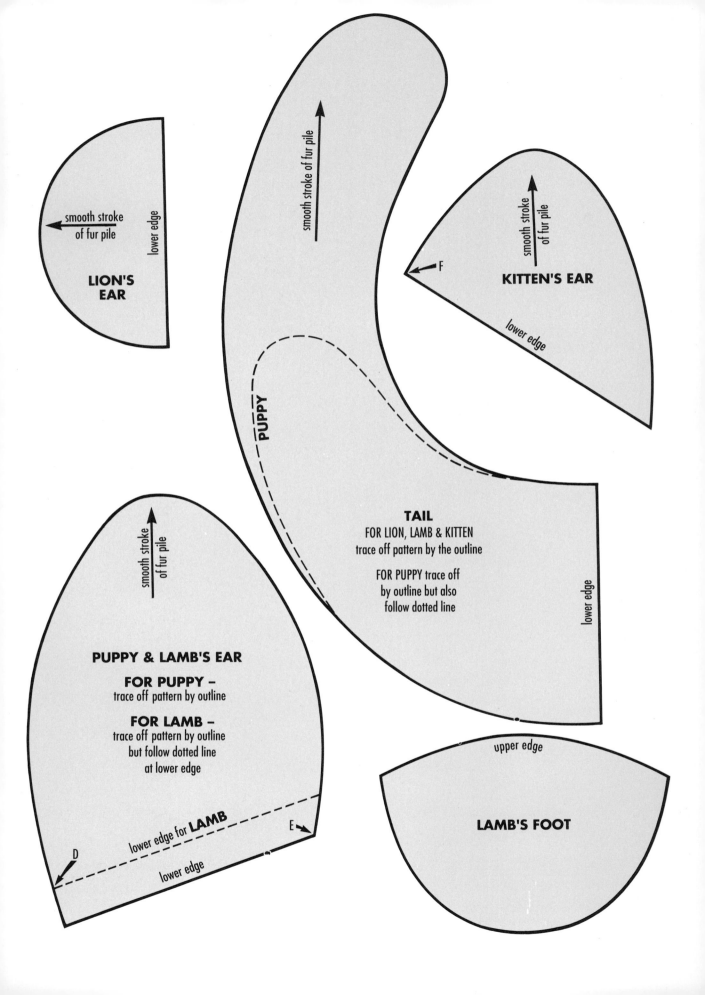

LION'S EAR

smooth stroke of fur pile

lower edge

smooth stroke of fur pile

PUPPY

KITTEN'S EAR

smooth stroke of fur pile

F

lower edge

TAIL
FOR LION, LAMB & KITTEN
trace off pattern by the outline

FOR PUPPY trace off
by outline but also
follow dotted line

lower edge

smooth stroke of fur pile

PUPPY & LAMB'S EAR

FOR PUPPY –
trace off pattern by outline

FOR LAMB –
trace off pattern by outline
but follow dotted line
at lower edge

lower edge for **LAMB**

D

E

lower edge

upper edge

LAMB'S FOOT

Wild West Show

Here's a cuddly quartet of soft toys – Cowboy Bill and Little Brave the Indian, plus their chubby, furry ponies. The dolls measure 40cm (16in) tall and the ponies are about 46cm (18in) from nose to tail.

THE PONIES

For each one you will need: 45cm (½yd) of fur fabric in white or dark fawn, 138cm (54in) wide; 600g (1¼lb) of stuffing; small ball, about 20g (¾oz) of thick knitting yarn (light grey or dark brown) for the mane and tail; oddments of felt for facial features; 1.80m (2yd) of braid about 1.5cm (⅝in) in width and four 2cm (¾in) diameter buttons for the bridle and reins; oddments of felt; ric-rac and braid for the saddle; dressmaker's graph paper, ruled into 5cm (2in) squares.

Notes: Patterns for facial features are given full size. Draw the other pattern shapes off the diagram square by square and mark on all details. When drawing the gusset pattern, have a folded edge of the graph paper at the dotted line when drawing, then cut out and open up to give full-sized pattern. Cut out all fur fabric pieces having 'smooth stroke' of fur pile in direction shown on pattern pieces. Cut the gusset across the *width* of fur fabric and test the direction of *smoothest* stroke across the width of your fur fabric before cutting, then cut out accordingly.

5mm (¼in) seams are allowed unless otherwise stated.

To make

Cut the pair of body pieces and one gusset from fur fabric. Mark points A and B on wrong side of all pieces with pencil. Mark all other lines (showing positions of legs, tail, mane, etc) on right side of fabric with long tacking stitches using coloured thread.

Join the body pieces from point A, over top of the head and round the back to point B, leaving a gap in seam as indicated. Stitch the gusset to underside of the body pieces, matching points A and B on both and also matching the leg positions marked with coloured threads. Turn body right side out and stuff firmly, then ladder-stitch the gap in the seam.

Cut eight leg pieces from fur fabric and join

them in pairs leaving the upper edges open. Turn right side out and stuff very firmly. Pin legs in place on the body having leg seams at positions marked with coloured threads on body and gusset seams. Sew the open upper raw edges of legs to body and gusset where they touch, adding more stuffing if necessary before completing sewing, to make the legs quite firm.

Cut four ear pieces from fur fabric and join them in pairs leaving lower edges open. Turn right side out and oversew lower edges together, pulling stitches to gather slightly. Sew ears in position as shown on the body pattern.

For the tail, cut eight 25cm (10in) lengths of yarn. Fold in half and sew them together at the folded centre. Sew the centre securely to position marked by coloured thread, then untwist and tease out the yarn strands to make finer strands.

For the mane, cut a 9x20cm (3½x8in) piece of card and wind yarn loosely round and round the 9cm (3½in) width all along the length. Wind yarn around the card again, back to the beginning. Now carefully pull out the card, machining through one looped edge of the yarn as you go. Machine again a little further down from the first line of stitching to make sure all the loops are caught. Snip through the other looped edges to make a fringe. Tease out the strands of yarn with a broad-toothed comb or a brush. The fringed

COWBOY BILL AND LITTLE BRAVE

Now Bill was a cowboy who lived in the West,
He rode on a pony that he loved the best,
A pony so fast, he was faster than light,
A pony so fast he was called Dynamite.

Little Brave was an Indian who lived in the West,
And he rode a pony that he loved the best,
A pony so fat he could only go slowly,
A pony so fat he was called Rolypoly!

mane will now be about twice as long as the length of card, so fold it in half and stitch again through all the looped edges. Pin the mane between the coloured threads along the head seam line, having the mane thrown over to one side of the head. Slip-stitch the stitched edge of the mane to the head seam, then turn the mane over to other side of head and sew in place again. Spread mane out evenly over back and forehead and trim off any long ends. Remove all coloured tacking threads.

Face
Lift the mane off the forehead and pin it back. Cut four eye pieces from felt (pale blue for the white pony, white for the brown pony). Join them in pairs, oversewing round the edges. Cut two pupils from black felt and sew to the eyes as shown on eye pattern. Cut two eyelids from flesh-coloured felt and sew to the eyes, having lower edges just overlapping top edges of the pupils. Using black thread stitch several times across the lower edges of the eyelids.

Pin the eyes in position placing them 2cm (³⁄₄in) apart and having the top edges about 3cm (1¼in) below the ears. Sew in place. Cut two nostrils (light brown felt for white pony, darker brown for the brown pony) and sew to the face 2cm (³⁄₄in) apart and 3.5cm (1³⁄₈in) below the eyes.

Trim fur fabric pile a little shorter below the nostrils and around chin area. For the mouth, cut a 5mmx4cm (¼x1½in) strip of black felt. Round off the ends and sew it in place making a shallow U-shape, about 3cm (1¼in) below the nostrils. Unpin the mane and stroke it down over eyes, then trim to length just above eyes.

Bridle and reins
When cutting the braid lengths, allow a little extra on each length for turning in or seaming the ends together.

For the noseband, cut a length of braid to fit round the face between nose and eyes and join the ends under chin. Cut another length to fit over head in front of ears and join the ends of this piece under head at the throat. Cut another length of braid to fit from side of noseband, over head behind ears to other side of noseband, then sew ends to noseband.

For the reins, cut a 57cm (22½in) length of braid. Turn in the ends and join to each side of noseband in the same position as the braid previously joined to noseband. Now sew a button to each of these positions, taking stitches into the fur fabric to secure firmly. Sew the remaining buttons to the other bridle pieces where they cross, just below ears.

Saddle
Cut a 12x25cm (4³⁄₄x10in) piece of felt. Round off the corners then stitch ric-rac braid round, 1cm (³⁄₈in) away from the edges. Put the saddle on the pony and sew braid to centre of one short edge on the wrong side of saddle. Take the braid under the pony and sew other end in place as for first end.

COWBOY BILL
You will need: 45cm (½yd) of pink cotton fabric 91cm (36in) wide; 250g (½lb) of stuffing; small ball of orange double-knitting yarn; oddments of checked fabric, plain fabric, fur fabric, felt and leather cloth (or alternatively felt); for the hat, a piece of felt measuring 40x55cm (16x22in) and oddment of braid; a small buckle (for a 1.5cm (⅝in) wide belt); two small buttons and two small snap fasteners; scraps of black and pink felt; red pencil; adhesive.

Notes: Draw the pattern shapes onto your graph paper in same way as for the ponies. Mark on all details. Use a small machine stitch when sewing the doll. 5mm (¼in) seams allowed on doll and boots; 1cm (³⁄₈in) seams and hems allowed on the garments unless otherwise stated.

To make the doll
Cut two head pieces from pink fabric and mark the longest mouth line (the one with the short lines at each end) on the right side of one head piece. On both head pieces mark the line indicated above neck edge with coloured tacking threads. Stitch over the mouth lines several times, using orange thread, to make a thick line.

Join the head pieces, with right sides together, leaving neck edges open. Clip the seam at neck and head curves. Turn head right side out and stuff very firmly, especially at the sides of face just above the neck. Stuff the neck firmly also, then lay head aside until later.

Cut two body pieces from pink fabric, placing pattern to fold in fabric each time as indicated. Mark dotted lines below the neck as for the head. Join the body pieces all round the edges leaving neck edges open and a gap in seam at side as shown on pattern. Clip seam at all curves especially between legs and clip at neck curves also.

Turn body right side out and make 1cm (⅜in) long clips in the raw neck edge. Turn in the neck edge as far as the tacked line. Slip neck edge of head inside neck edge of body until the tacked lines meet, having side seams of head and body matching. Pin the neck edges in this position, then slip-stitch neck edge of body securely to head. Remove the tacking threads.

Stuff the legs through gap in side seam then stuff body firmly, taking care to push stuffing well into neck. Ladder-stitch the gap in seam.

Cut two pairs of arm pieces from pink fabric and join them in pairs leaving the upper edges open. Trim seams round hands and thumbs. Turn right side out and stuff arms firmly to within 2cm (¾in) of the upper edges. Turn in and oversew upper edges together, pulling stitches to gather tightly. Sew the arms to each side of body 2.5cm (1in) down from the neck. Sew a snap fastener half to the palm of each hand.

Cut cowboy's nose from pink felt and stick to the face about 2cm (¾in) above the lower curve of the mouth. Cut two cowboy eyes from black felt and work a small highlight on each one using white thread. Glue the eyes to face 2.5cm (1in) apart. Colour the cheeks with red pencil.

For the hair, cut a 5x26cm (2x10in) piece of card and wind yarn loosely round and round the 5cm (2in) width all along length. Now carefully pull out the card, machining through one looped edge of the yarn as you go. Machine again a little further down from first line of stitching to make sure all the loops are caught. Snip through the other looped edges to make a fringe.

Now pin the stitched edge of fringe to head, having the cut ends of strands just above the eyes at front and about 3cm (1¼in) above the neck at back. Do not sew the hair in place at this stage.

THE CLOTHES
Boots
Cut two pairs of boot pieces from leather cloth or felt. Join them in pairs taking 5mm (¼in) seams and leaving the upper edges open. Trim seams close to stitching line and turn right side out. Stuff the toes and heels firmly, then push the ends of the legs right inside the boots, matching leg and boot seams. Sew the upper edges of boots to legs.

Shirt
Cut two shirt pieces from checked fabric placing the edge indicated to fold in fabric each time. Cut one piece open at the fold line for fronts of shirt. Join fronts to back at the shoulder edges, then the side and underarm edges. Clip seams at underarms as indicated.

Take narrow hems on the wrist and lower edges. Bind the neck edge with a 2cm (¾in) wide straight strip of the shirt fabric to neaten, taking narrow seams. Put the shirt on the doll, turn in the left front edge 5mm (¼in) and lap it 1cm (⅜in) over the right front edge, then slip-stitch in place.

Pants
Cut one pair of pants pieces from fur fabric and one pair from brown felt. Join the pairs together at centre edges then trim the seams. Join the fur fabric pieces to the felt pieces at sides, then join the inside leg edges and trim all seams.

Turn in lower edges and hem. Turn right side out. Put the pants on the doll and slip-stitch the raw waist edge to the doll through shirt fabric, making sure that the shirt is well tucked in before sewing.

Belt
Cut a strip of leather cloth or felt 1.5cm (⅝in) wide by 36cm (14¼in) in length. Attach one end to the buckle, then put belt on the doll at waist edge of the pants. Pierce a hole in belt to fasten at centre front, then trim the end into a V shape. Secure the belt to shirt with a little adhesive spread underneath the belt.

Neckerchief
Cut a 26cm (10¼in) square of thin fabric and fray out all the edges a little. Fold the square corner to opposite corner and tie round the doll's neck as illustrated, securing the knot with a stitch or two. Now sew the two small buttons to centre front of the shirt.

Hat
Cut two hat crown pieces from felt, placing the edge indicated on pattern to fold each time. Join the pieces leaving lower edges open. Trim seam. Bring the side seams of hat crown together then stitch across the top of the hat from front to back about 3cm (1¼in) below the top edge. Trim off felt above the stitching line. Turn right side out.

Cut two hat brim pieces placing edge indicated on pattern to fold in felt each time. Join centre back edges of each brim piece taking a tiny seam. Place the brim pieces wrong sides together, matching seams, then stitch them together close to the outer and inner edges.

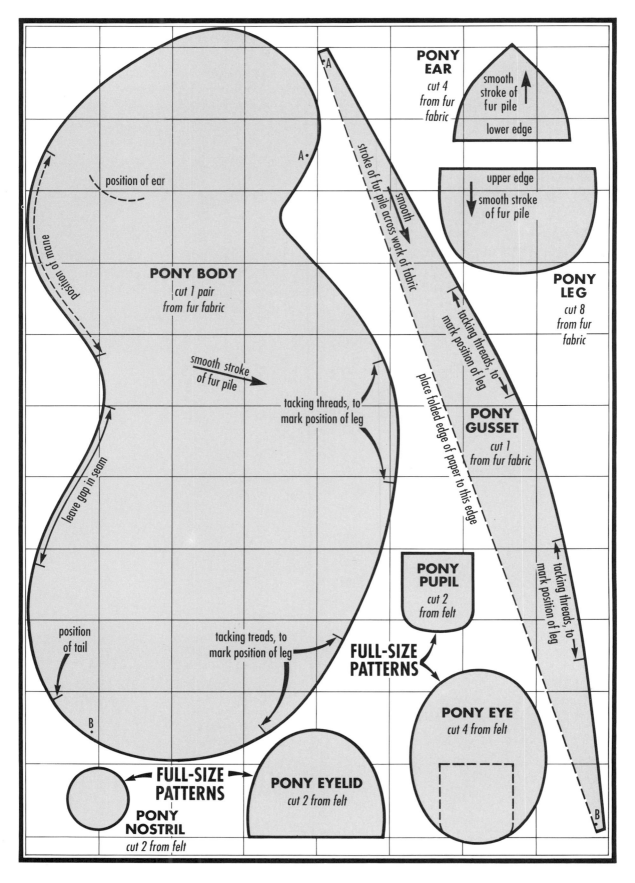

PONY EAR
cut 4 from fur fabric

smooth stroke of fur pile

lower edge

upper edge

smooth stroke of fur pile

PONY LEG
cut 8 from fur fabric

position of ear

PONY BODY
cut 1 pair from fur fabric

position of mane

smooth stroke of fur pile

stroke of fur pile across work of fabric

smooth

tacking threads, to mark position of leg

place folded edge of paper to this edge

PONY GUSSET
cut 1 from fur fabric

tacking threads, to mark position of leg

leave gap in seam

tacking threads, to mark position of leg

position of tail

tacking treads, to mark position of leg

PONY PUPIL
cut 2 from felt

FULL-SIZE PATTERNS

FULL-SIZE PATTERNS

PONY EYE
cut 4 from felt

PONY NOSTRIL
cut 2 from felt

PONY EYELID
cut 2 from felt

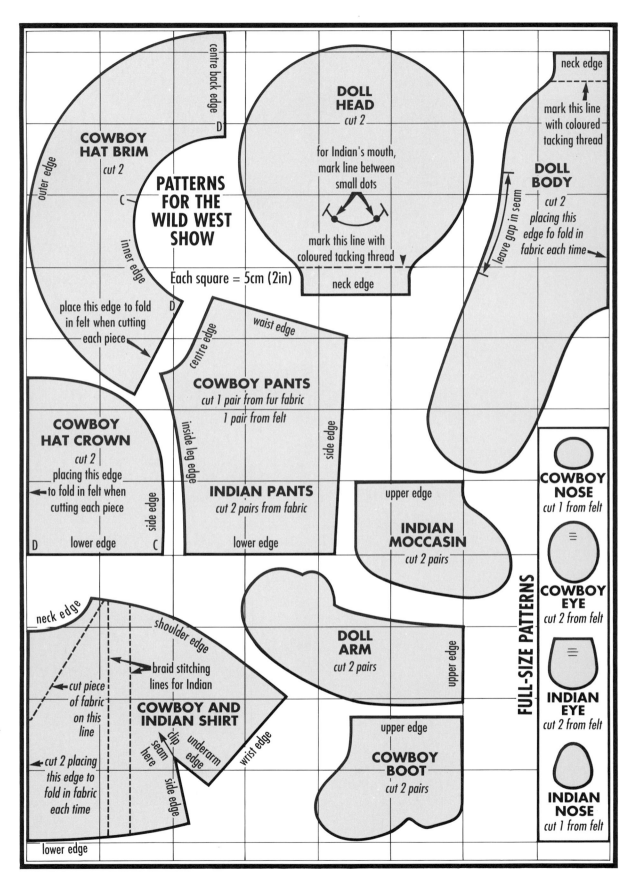

COWBOY HAT BRIM
cut 2

outer edge

inner edge

centre back edge

D

C

D

place this edge to fold in felt when cutting each piece

PATTERNS FOR THE WILD WEST SHOW

Each square = 5cm (2in)

DOLL HEAD
cut 2

for Indian's mouth, mark line between small dots

mark this line with coloured tacking thread

neck edge

neck edge

mark this line with coloured tacking thread

DOLL BODY
cut 2
placing this edge to fold in fabric each time

leave gap in seam

COWBOY HAT CROWN
cut 2
placing this edge to fold in felt when cutting each piece

side edge

D   lower edge   C

centre edge

waist edge

inside leg edge

side edge

COWBOY PANTS
cut 1 pair from fur fabric
1 pair from felt

INDIAN PANTS
cut 2 pairs from fabric

lower edge

upper edge

INDIAN MOCCASIN
cut 2 pairs

neck edge

shoulder edge

braid stitching lines for Indian

cut piece of fabric on this line

cut 2 placing this edge to fold in fabric each time

COWBOY AND INDIAN SHIRT

clip seam here

underarm edge

side edge

wrist edge

lower edge

DOLL ARM
cut 2 pairs

upper edge

upper edge

COWBOY BOOT
cut 2 pairs

FULL-SIZE PATTERNS

COWBOY NOSE
cut 1 from felt

COWBOY EYE
cut 2 from felt

INDIAN EYE
cut 2 from felt

INDIAN NOSE
cut 1 from felt

120

Now sew the inner edge of brim to lower edge of hat crown, matching points C and D, taking a 5mm (¼in) seam and having right sides of both together. Place the hat on cowboy's head overlapping top edge of the hair. Adjust position of hair if necessary to hang down as illustrated. Remove the hat and sew stitched edge of hair to the head as pinned. Stuff top of hat, then place it on the head again and sew to head through seam line at lower edge of crown, adding more stuffing if necessary. Sew braid round the hat for hatband. Turn up the brim at centre front and back and catch invisibly to the crown.

Place the cowboy on the pony and pin the reins to his hands. Sew other halves of snap fasteners to reins as pinned (they should be positioned about 20cm (8in) away from each noseband button).

THE INDIAN

You will need: 45cm (½yd) of light fawn cotton fabric 91cm (36in) wide; 250g (½lb) of stuffing; a 20g (¾oz) ball of black double-knitting yarn and short length of black tape, for hair; oddments of yellow fabric, geometric patterned fabric, braid and felt; 80cm (⅞yd) of fancy narrow braid for binding hair; 1.20m (1¼yd) fancy braid about 2cm (¾in) wide for trimming the shirt and pants; 90cm (1yd) fringed trimming; two small snap fasteners; scraps of black and brown felt; red pencil; adhesive.

Notes: As for Cowboy Bill.

To make the doll

Make the basic doll exactly as for Cowboy Bill (using the fawn fabric), except for the face and hair. Stitch the shorter mouth line between the *small dots* shown on the head pattern.

Cut the Indian's nose from brown felt and the eyes from black felt. Work highlights on the eyes and stick eyes and nose in place as for Cowboy Bill, then colour cheeks with pencil.

For the hair, cut a 16cm (6¼in) length of black tape, then cut yarn into 46cm (18in) lengths and stitch the centres of yarn lengths to the tape to cover it, leaving 1cm (⅜in) at each end of the tape uncovered. Turn in the ends of tape and pin one end, tape side down, to doll's forehead 4cm (1½in) above the eyes. Pin the other end to centre back of head above the neck. Sew hair to head along the stitching line. Now smooth down the yarn

strands, gathering them to each side of the head, at the same time spreading adhesive on the head to hold the strands in place. Tie a strand of yarn tightly round each bunch of hair level with the mouth then sew the tied bunches to the head.

To bind the hair, cut the narrow braid into two equal lengths and wind braid tightly round hair, starting where each bunch is sewn to head. Sew the ends of braids in place. Now trim the ends of the hair to even lengths. Sew a length of wider braid round the head for the headband, joining ends at centre back.

THE CLOTHES

Moccasins

Make and sew in place in same way as cowboy boots.

Pants

Cut two pairs of pants pieces from yellow fabric. Join the pairs at side edges enclosing fringed trimming in seams between the pieces and having raw edges of fabric and top edges of fringe level. On the right side of each piece sew a strip of braid alongside the fringe taking care that on each piece, braid will be at *front* of the pants when pieces are sewn together. Now join the pants pieces at the centre edges and clip curves in seams. Join the inside leg edges, then hem lower edges. Turn right side out. Put the pants on doll and slip-stitch raw waist edge to the doll.

Shirt

Cut two shirt pieces from yellow fabric as for Cowboy Bill. The piece which is cut open at the centre fold will be *back* pieces of shirt for the Indian.

On the front shirt piece, stitch two vertical strips of braid (to match the pants) at positions shown. Cut a piece of fabric (with geometric design) to the V-shape shown at neck of shirt pattern, placing pattern to fold as when cutting the shirt pieces. Sew raw edges of fabric to shirt front. Sew on fringed trimming along the V-line of fabric to cover the raw edges.

Now sew braid strips to the shirt back pieces to match the front. Join shirt seams, hem wrist and lower edges as for cowboy shirt. Bind neck edge as for cowboy shirt but use a 3cm (1¼in) wide strip of fabric. Sew fringed trimming to lower edge of shirt. Sew braid round the wrist edges.

Put shirt on doll and overlap and sew back edges in place as for Cowboy Bill's shirt.

Clown

This 56cm (22in) high doll is made mostly from straight strips of fabric and stockinette, with simple trace-off patterns for the pants, cap, feet and hands.

You will need: 40cm (½yd) of 91cm (36in) wide gingham fabric; 50cm (⅝yd) of 91cm (36in) wide printed fabric; oddments of the following: pink stockinette and white fabric, fabric for lining the pants, red and black felt for facial features, also felt for braces, thin Polyester wadding, narrow ribbon or tape, braid for trimming sleeves; a 17cm (6¾in) length of 2cm (¾in) wide elastic; 600g (1¼lb) of stuffing; 4cm (1½in) length of Velcro hook and loop fastener; red pencil; a 24x30cm (9½x12in) piece of felt for feet; a 20g (¾oz) ball of yellow double-knitting yarn and a pair of 3¾mm (No 9, USA 4) knitting needles for hair; adhesive.

Notes: 5mm (¼in) seams are allowed on all pieces unless otherwise stated. Trace patterns off the page and mark on all details. Note that pants pattern is printed over two pages; trace off both sections and join them at the dot and dash lines indicated. Knitting abbreviations: K, knit; st, stitch.

Legs
Cut two pairs of foot pieces from felt. Join them in pairs at centre front edges for a little of the seam only. For each leg, cut a 15x19cm (6x7½in) strip of gingham fabric. Join one long edge of each strip to the ankle edge of each foot. Now join remainder of foot seams and also short edges of legs. Trim seams round feet. Turn and stuff firmly to within 5cm (2in) of tops of legs, then stuff lightly. Stitch raw edges of each leg together, having leg seam at centre.

Head and Body
For the head, cut a 21x26cm (8¼x10¼in) strip of stockinette, having the most stretch in fabric going across the longest measurement.

For the body, cut an 18x37cm (7x14½in) strip of gingham. Gather one long edge to fit one long edge of the stockinette strip. Stitch in place with right sides together and raw edges level. Now join short edges of body and head strips, to form the centre back seam.

PERHAPS

Perhaps I'll be a circus clown,
And dress in funny clothes,
A silly hat upon my head,
A red nose on my nose.

Perhaps I'll be a circus clown,
Paint black stuff on my eyes,

And do the splits and somersaults,
And throw some custard pies.

Perhaps I'll be a circus clown,
'Cause sometimes in the bath,
I try to catch the bubbles,
And my mummy starts to laugh!

Turn in the remaining raw edge of body and tack. Turn right side out and bring these edges together with seam at centre back position. Slip the upper raw edges of legs inside lower edge of body and tack, then stitch across through all thicknesses. Stuff body, then stuff head to measure about 44cm (17¼in) around. Gather the stockinette 1cm (⅜in) away from top raw edge, pull up tightly turning in raw edge, then fasten off.

Tie the length of narrow ribbon or tape very tightly round the neck at seam line. Knot, then trim ends and sew these ends to neck to neaten.

Arms

Place a double thickness of stockinette between two layers of white fabric. Use the hand pattern to cut two pairs of hand pieces from the four-thickness fabric, taking care to have most stretch in stockinette in direction shown on the pattern. Join hand pieces in pairs starting at wrist edge at the side opposite to thumb and stitching only a small portion of the seam.

For each sleeve, cut a 14x24cm (5½x9½in) strip of gingham. Gather one long edge of each sleeve to fit wrist edge of each hand. Sew in place with right sides together and raw edges level. Join remainder of hand seams and short edges of sleeves. Trim seams around hands. Turn right side out. Stuff hands firmly, then sleeves lightly. Turn in top raw edge of each sleeve, bring together to close, having seam at centre. Gather through all thicknesses at turned-in edges, pull up tightly, then fasten off. Sew braid round wrist edges of sleeves. Sew the gathered tops of sleeves to sides of body 3cm (1⅛in) down from the neck. Catch the sleeve seams to body 3cm (1⅛in) below the gathers.

Pants

Cut two pairs of pants pieces from printed fabric. Join each pair at the side edges and press the seams open. Split the wadding by pulling it apart to give thinnest layers. Place the pants pieces right side up on the wadding and tack them to wadding round the edges. Cut out the wadding level with edges of fabric.

Now join the pants pieces to each other at the centre edges. Stitch twice at curves to reinforce, then trim seams here. Bring the centre seams together, then join the inside leg edges of each leg. Turn pants right side out.

Make up the lining in same way as pants omitting the wadding. Leave lining wrong side out and slip it inside pants. Tack the waist and ankle edges of pants and lining together. For the waistband, cut a 6x42cm (2⅜x16½in) strip of gingham and join short ends. Gather the waist edge of pants to fit one long edge of the waistband and stitch in place, with right sides together and raw edges level. Tack ends of elastic inside the waistband, level with the side seams of pants. Turn in the remaining raw edge of waistband and slip-stitch in place over the waist seam. Stitch ends of elastic in place through both thicknesses of the waistband.

For the ankle bands, cut two 6x27cm (2⅜x10¾in) strips of gingham. Gather the ankle edges of pants and sew on the bands as for waistband ignoring reference to elastic.

Braces

Cut two 6x28cm (2⅜x11in) strips of felt. Join long edges of each one and round off seam at one short edge. Trim at rounded corners, turn right side out and press. Sew the open ends to inside of pants back waistband at an angle, so that braces cross over at the back to pass over the shoulders.

For the buttons, cut two 2cm (¾in) diameter circles of felt and sew them to rounded ends of braces, then work a cross stitch at centre of each one. Sew small strips of Velcro to ends of braces and to front of waistband on the right side.

Face

Use red thread to work a U-shape for mouth in small back stitches 4cm (1½in) up from the neck. Work back along the mouth, oversewing through each stitch. Cut the nose and eyes from felt as stated on the patterns. Work a highlight on each eye with white thread as shown on pattern. Glue nose in place 2cm (¾in) above the mouth. Pin eyes at each side of the nose placing them 3cm (1⅛in) apart. Use pencil to mark straight lines at side, upper and lower edges of the eyes. Remove the eyes and work long stitches along the lines in black thread. Glue the eyes in place. Colour the cheeks with red pencil.

Hair

Cast on 84 sts and work the looped pattern as follows:

1st row: K 1; * insert right-hand needle K-wise into next st, place first 2 fingers of left hand at back of st, wind yarn anti-clockwise round needle and fingers 4 times, then round tip of right-hand needle only, draw through the 5 loops; repeat from * to last st; K 1.

Next row is the cast-off row, (cast off loosely): K 1; * K 5 together, pass first st on right-hand needle over second st thus casting it off; repeat from * to last st; K 1, then cast off last st. Join the row ends and lay hair aside.

Cap

Cut four cap pieces from printed fabric as directed on pattern. Tack each one to split wadding in same way as for the pants. Join the pieces in pairs at one side edge then join the pairs at remaining side edges. Bind the lower edge of cap with a 6x49cm (2⅜x19¼in) strip of gingham. Place the lower edge of the band over the cast-off edge of hair and stitch in place. For cap bobble, cut, gather and stuff a 10cm (4in) diameter circle of gingham. Sew to top of cap. Stuff top of cap and sew to head through the hair strip just below cap band.

Neck Frill

Cut a 12x64cm (4¾x25in) strip of printed fabric and join the long edges. Tack across one short end. Turn right side out pushing short tacked edge through. Remove tacking and press the strip with the seam at centre back. Turn in raw edges at the ends and join the ends neatly. Gather up one long edge tightly round doll's neck and fasten off. Space out the gathers evenly and sew them to neck.

FULL-SIZE PATTERNS FOR THE CLOWN

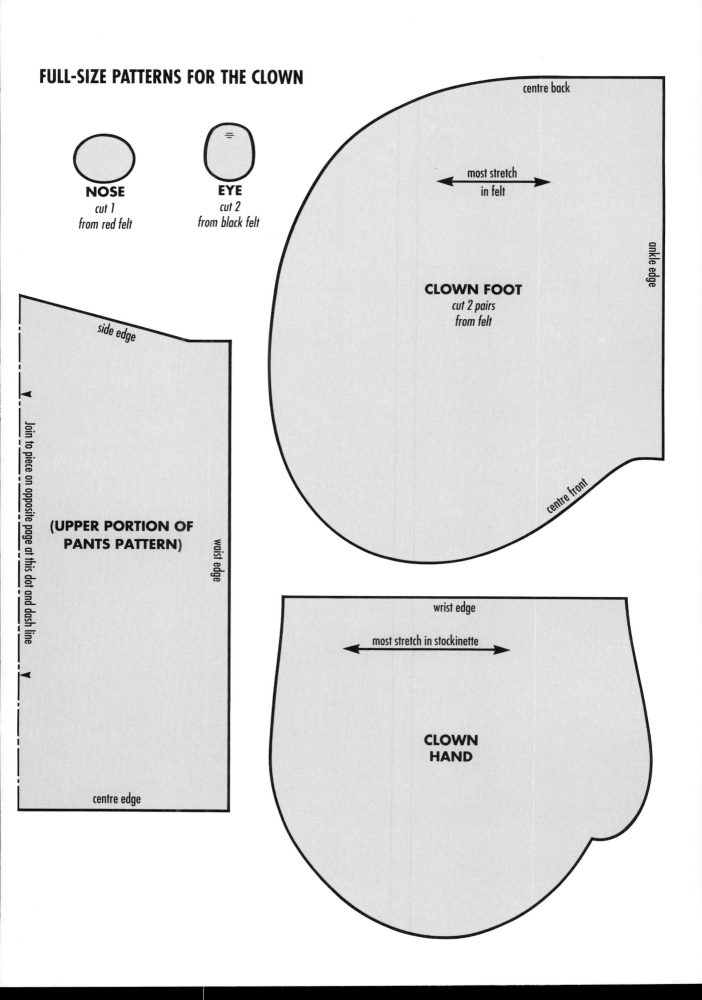

NOSE
cut 1
from red felt

EYE
cut 2
from black felt

centre back

most stretch
in felt

ankle edge

CLOWN FOOT
cut 2 pairs
from felt

centre front

side edge

Join to piece on opposite page at this dot and dash line

(UPPER PORTION OF PANTS PATTERN)

waist edge

centre edge

wrist edge

most stretch in stockinette

CLOWN HAND

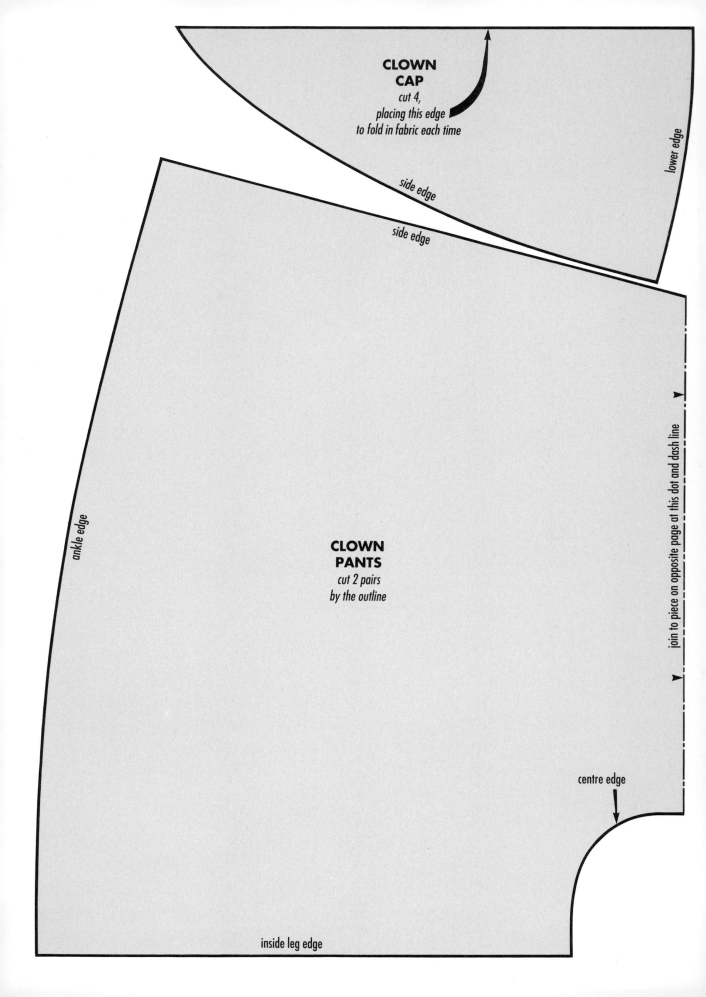

CLOWN CAP
cut 4,
placing this edge
to fold in fabric each time

side edge

lower edge

side edge

ankle edge

CLOWN PANTS
cut 2 pairs
by the outline

join to piece on opposite page at this dot and dash line

centre edge

inside leg edge

STOCKISTS

The UK stockists listed will supply by mail order to the USA, Australia, etc. You can telephone or, better still, write for details, enclosing a stamped self-addressed envelope for a reply.

For Care Bears and other fur fabrics, toy-filling, felt, plastic granules for bean-bags, and many other toy-making and craft materials:

Beckfoot Mill
Prince Street
Dudley Hill
Bradford BD4 6HQ
Tel (0274) 651065

For Care Bears and other fur fabrics, polyester toy filling; felt, and many other toy- making and craft materials:

Griffin Fabrics Ltd
The Craft Centre
97 Claremont
Street
Aberdeen AB1 6QR
Tel (0224) 580798

For Care Bears and other fur fabrics, toy-filling, Binca embroidery fabric, glues, felt, and many other toy-making materials:

The Handicraft
Shop
Northgate
Canterbury
Kent CT1 1BE
Tel (0227) 451188

USA

All materials used in this book will be readily available from your local supplier, but if necessary, the following mail order sources can supply fur fabrics, etc:

The Crafty Teddy Inc
168 Seventh Street
Brooklyn
New York 11215

Merrily Doll Supply Co
8542 Ranchito Avenue
Panorama City
California 91402

ENGLISH – AMERICAN GLOSSARY

Fasten off	Secure end of thread
Fur fabric	Fake fur
Fuse wire	Very thin wire
Guipure flowers	Daisy lace, flower trim, flower decals
Iron-on interfacing	Non-woven fusible interfacing
Plasticine	Reusable modelling clay
Polyester stuffing	Polyester fibrefill
Polyester wadding	Polyester quilt batting
Ric-rac	Rickrack
Snap fasteners	Snaps
Sticky tape	Transparent adhesive tape for sticking on paper
Stockinette	Cotton knit fabric
Strong thread	Buttonhole twist
Tack	Baste
UHU glue	Tacky glue or Slomons

INDEX

Adhesive, 8, 11
Animals, for zoo rug, 87–9, *90–1*
Arms, 16, 26, 34, *39, 41*, 47, 50, 61, 63, 78, *80*, 82, 104, 106, 118, 123–4
Balls, 106
Beads, 8, 56, 58, 60, 61
Beans, 101, 102
Belts, 32, 118
Beard, 48, *49*
Blazer, 52–4
Bodies, 15, *17*, 22, *23*, 26, 33–4, *39, 40*, 47, 50, 63, *67*, 75, 77, *79*, 82, 96, 98, 102, 104, 107, 108, *111, 112*, 115, 116, *119*, 122–3
Boots, 118
Bo-Peep, 92–4
Bows, 11
Boy Blue, 94
Braces, 124
Braid, 11, 31, 32, 62, 75, 78, 92, 96, 101, 115, 116, 121, 122
Bridle, 116
Broderie anglaise, 14, 16, 101
Buckles, 32, 107
Buttons, 8, 26, 33, 75, 101, 115

Camels, 7, 20–4, *21*
Capes, 30, 32
Caps, 65, 82, 124, *126*
Car, 74
Caravan, 74
Card, 33, 45, 56, 101
Chimps, 96–100
Claws, 58
Clowns, 106, 122–6
Coat, 52
Compasses, 8, 10, 56
Cotton wool, 104
Cowboy Bill, 116–18, 121
Crab, 58
Cravat, 54
Crook, 94

Dolls, 11–12, 33–49, *35, 45*, 75–82, 92–5, 116–26, *120*
Dowelling, 100
Dresses, *28*, 30–1, 37–8, *42–3*, 78, *80*, 92; Wedding, 75, 78
Ears, 14, *18, 23*, 24, 51, *99*, 108–10 *passim 114*, 115
Eyes, 13, 15, *17*, 22, *22*, 24, 26, 51, 77, 89, 107, *119*

Fabric, 11–12, 14, 26, 33, 45, 56, 62, 75, 83, 92, 96, 116, 121, 122; fur, 9, 10, *11*, 14, 20, 24, 25, 45, 48, 50, 75, 78, 83, 84, 86, 107–10, 115–16; leather, 116, 118
Faces, 11, 13, 22, *22*, 24, 34, 48, 51, 61, 64, 75, 77, *99*, 116, 124
Fairy, 104
Feet, 11, *11*, 15, *19*, 60, *66*, 109, *114, 125*
Felt, 11, *11*, 14, 21, 24, 26, 33, 45, 50, 63, 68, 75, 89, 96, 115, 116, 121, 122
Fish, 60

Flowers, 56, 58, 101, 104
Fraying, 11

Garland, Christmas, 102–4

Hair, 34, 48, 61, 65, 77–8, 82, 89, 118, 124
Hands, *19*, 47, *49, 66, 99*, 124, *125*
Harness, 24
Hats, *28*, 38, 48, 54, 94, *99*, 100, *105*, 106, 118
Headband, 61
Head-dress, 75, 78
Heads, 14, *17, 19*, 26, 33–4, *39, 40*, 47, 50, 63, *67*, 75, 77, *79, 80*, 82, 96, 98, *99*, 102, *113*, 116, 122
Hoods, *28*, 30, 32
Horn, 94, *95*
Humpty Dumpty, 62–7

Indian, 121
Interfacing, 9, 63, 68, 101, 102

Jacket, *81*, 82

Kapok, 9, 12
Kitten, 110

Lace, 14, 26, 30, 75, 92
Laces, 11, 21, 24
Lamb, 108–10
Legs, 15–16, *19*, 22, *23*, 26, 34, 36, *41*, 50, 58, 60, 63, 75, 78, *81*, 82, 98, 122
Limpet, 60
Lion, 110

Mane, 110, 115
Measurements, 9, 56
Mermaid, 57, 61
Mouth, 13, 26, 110

Neckerchief, 118
Necklace, 61
Needles, darning, *12*, 13
Nightcap, *29*, 20
Nightshirt, 26–7, *29*
Nose, 26, 108, 110, *113*, 118
Nostrils, 24

Octopus, 60

Pantaloons, 36, *43, 44*
Pants, 16, *18, 29*, 32, 52, 64, *66*, 118, 121, 124
Paper, graph, 10; tracing, 9–10
Patterns, 9–10
Paws, 51
Pebbles, 60
Petticoat, 36
Pins, 8
Pipe cleaners, 94
Polyester, 8–9, 12
Ponies, 115–16, *119*
Prince, 78–82
Puppy, 108

Reins, 116
Ribbon, 11, 14, 30–1, 45, 63, 75, 92, 101, 107, 122
Rug, zoo, 83–91
Ruler, 8

Saddle, 116
Safety, 8, 13, 101
Santa Claus, 47–8; Mrs, 48
Scissors, 8
Scarf, 52
Sea creatures, 56–61 *see also individual headings*
Seams, 12
Sewing machine, 8
Sheeting, 11
Shells, 56–8
Shirt, 82, 121
Shoes, 34, 36, 47–8, *49*, 78, *81*, 93, 98, *98*
Skirts, 16, 48, 93–4, 104
Sleeping beauty, 75–8
Slippers, 31
Socks, towelling, 83, 87–9, 96, 101, 102
Starfish, 60–1
Stitch, ladder, 13, *13*
Stockinette, 12, 45, 47, 56, 61, 89, 92, 122
Stocking, 102, *105*
Stockists, 127
Stretch, of material, 11–12
Stuffing, 8–9, 12, 16, 22, 26, 33, 45, 50, 56, 62, 68, 75, 83, 92, 96, 101, 107, 115, 116, 121, 122
Suit, 98, 106

Tail, 22, *23*, 61, 108–10, *113*–15 *passim*
Tape, 33, 121
Tape measure, 8
Teddies, 7, 14–19, 25–32, *25*, 50–5, 101–6; bean-bag, 102; Cinderbearella, 30–2; Little Bear Riding Hood, 30; Robear-in-hood, 32; Wee Teddy Winkie, 26–30
Thimble, 8
Thread, 8, 13
Tinsel, 101
Towelling, 83, 86–9 *passim*, 96, 101
Tracing, 9–10
Trapeze, 100
Tunic, 32
Tweezers, 8

Van, 68, 74
Vehicles, 68–74, *70–3*
Velcro, 9, 14, 56, 96, 100, 122

Wand, 104, 106
Windows, 68, *70–3*
Wings, 104
Wire, 8

Yarn, knitting, 9, 21, 24, 26, 33, 34, 45, 50, 56, 61, 63, 75, 82, 101, 102, 107, 115, 118, 121